POETIC VOYAGES
STRATHCLYDE

Edited by Dave Thomas

First published in Great Britain in 2001 by
YOUNG WRITERS
Remus House,
Coltsfoot Drive,
Peterborough, PE2 9JX
Telephone (01733) 890066

HB ISBN 0 75433 222 5
SB ISBN 0 75433 223 3

FOREWORD

Young Writers was established in 1991 with the aim to promote creative writing in children, to make reading and writing poetry fun.

This year once again, proved to be a tremendous success with over 88,000 entries received nationwide.

The Poetic Voyages competition has shown us the high standard of work and effort that children are capable of today. It is a reflection of the teaching skills in schools, the enthusiasm and creativity they have injected into their pupils shines clearly within this anthology.

The task of selecting poems was therefore a difficult one but nevertheless, an enjoyable experience. We hope you are as pleased with the final selection in *Poetic Voyages Strathclyde* as we are.

CONTENTS

Craig Anderson	50
Darren Anderson	50
Laura-Jane McCallum	51
Seona McNaughton	52
Hannah Colville	53
Andrew Lazarus	54
Kelly Brodrick	54
Colin Millar	55
Katie Conley	56
Jennifer McMillan	57
Andrew Henderson	57
Claire McFadzean	58
Matthew Turner	58
Cheryl Brown	59

Forehill Primary School

Fiona Douglas	59
Jamie Edgar	60
Kirsty Mackie	60
Darren Swan	61
Neil Stoddart	62
Ross Clarkson	62
Craig MacMorland	63
Emma Cairns	64
Stewart McKie	65
Aya Musbahi	66
Rachel Anderson	66
Fiona Rosamond	67
Elaine Stoddart	67
Nicola Leonard	68
Kevin McHarg	68
Stephanie Leske	69
Darren McCann	70
Ian Chapman	70
Sarah Sargent	71
Stephanie Britt	71
Rachel McCutcheon	72
Craig Maxwell	72

Scott Cassidy	96
Callum Dunlop	96
Eilidh Hollow	97
David Moore	97
Tobias Kolb	97
Calum Atkinson	98
Andrew Young	98
Gillian Geoghan	99
Brogan Murphy	100
Scott Monaghan	100
Heather McCallum	101
Luke Sargent	101
Robbie Hunter	102
Samantha Lee	102
Rebecca Gibson	103
Hayley Swan	103
Neil Shankland	104
Michelle Jayne Nicol	104
Steven Morrison	104
Laura MacDuff	105
Craig McGhee	105
Alana Rachel Watt	105
Lyndsay McCabe	106
Connor McPherson	106
Garry Johnston	107
Stuart Ritchie	107
Greg Templeton	108
Lesley McIntyre	109
Greg Paterson	109
Rosie Eggo	110
Melanie Stobie	110

Inveraray Primary School

Bruce MacDonald	110
Jamie Divers	111
Kate Stronach	111

Sandbank Primary School

Liam Baird	147
Ryan Scott	148
Gemma Dorward	148
Jennifer Barron	149
Lesley Skewis	149
Tom Howard	150
Cara Phillips	150
Daniel Fairclough	150
Scott Ferguson	151
Allan Holland	151
Zoe Gray	152
Christine Alder	152
Andrew Kuchmeister	153
Alexis Ritchie	153

Taynuilt School

Kirsty Gillies	154
Ruth Cameron	155
Jamie Aitken	156
Hannah Matheson	156
Mair McTighe	157
Callum Nicol	158
Kirsten Bergant	158
Toni Ann Cooke	159
Fiona Rawcliffe	159
Jessica Anna Dalgleish	160
Liam McGukin	160
George Holmyard	161
Steven Parr	161
Mairi Campbell	162
Nina Currie	162
Alexander McDonald	163

Tayvallich Primary School

Christopher Murdanaigum	163
Sarah Shackleton	164

The Poems

THE SAFARI PARK

Is a wonderful place.

Curious cheetahs
Hungrily watch as we pass
Monkeys clamber over the car
Lions lazily bathe in the sun.

Inside we enjoy a scary death slide
That lands in a ball pit.

Fun! Laughter! Face painting!
Helter-skelter! Pets Corner!
What a wonderful time at the safari park.

Stephanie McFarlane (10)
Auchinleck Primary School

LISA

I remember
With affection
My furry little friend.
She yawned and smiled
At my sleepy face,
She even tried to climb out of her cage.
My favourite friend is now
Gracefully waiting
For me in the clouds.

Kirsty Graham (10)
Auchinleck Primary School

MY WEIRD FAMILY

I have a brother
I don't want another,
I'd like a little sister
Not bad, like Christopher.

My mum, she plays
A drum
She is quite smart
Not good at art.

My dad he's
Sometimes mad
He has a car and drives on tar.

I have a nanna who
Eats bananas
She cannot swim, she's not
That thin.

As for my dog, he eats
Like a hog
His name is Buster, he likes
Toffee clusters.

My first cat has
A mat
He is all fluffy and eats rudely.

My second cat is sort of fat,
His colour is ginger, he tries to
Eat my finger.

Last there is me,
I can swim in the sea,
But most precious of all
Is my family.

Stacey-Lee Stewart (10)
Auchinleck Primary School

WITCHES

Witches! Witches!
You don't need stitches
At the hospital.
Were you eaten by a cannibal?
No! It was witches
Got me in stitches.

Who needs witches?
They cause mayhem
Are a lot of bother
Just like my brother.
Who needs brothers?
Not me!

Stephanie Baird (10)
Auchinleck Primary School

MY MUM IS LIKE A BIRD

My mum is like a bird,
She glides through the air.
She sings very sweetly.
She is very peaceful
And she is my
Mum!

Kirsty Murray (10)
Ayr Grammar Primary School

SNOW

I am excited,
I think of fun.
I see footprints and an old man.
Snowmen to build,
Snowball fights with my friends.
Christmas toys to play with,
Many snow angels to make.
Go singing Christmas carols,
Visit my family for a while.
Have a hot chocolate to warm me,
See a little robin and feed it.
Go to the shop with my money
And buy peanuts,
Then winter ends and do does fun.

Steven Woods (9)
Ayr Grammar Primary School

BACK TO SCHOOL

Oh no! It's school tomorrow.
I must get my school bag ready.
Horrible maths.
Fun art.
I won't be able to sleep tonight.
Oh my reading book, where is it?
I've lost it.
I'd better find it or I am in trouble!
I walked really slowly.
I was nearly late!
Wait a minute, Katrina's back.
Happy new year everyone.

Sue Currie (8)
Ayr Grammar Primary School

SNOW

It's snowing here,
Christmas is here,
Snowball fights,
And snowmen too,
Trees bare,
Mum's making pie,
We're having a Christmas party,
It's freezing cold,
The snow's going on my face,
The wind is whistling,
The old man trudging up the garden,
Snow, cold as ice,
Birds singing on the wall,
Footsteps in the snow,
The snow's going pitter-patter
On the ground.

Kirsty Linton (9)
Ayr Grammar Primary School

GOING BACK TO SCHOOL

At the last night of the holiday
I was thinking about school,
About my friends and the staff
Getting ready to go to work.
I wish the holiday would last forever
We can't watch TV,
Our friends can't come over,
But when you get to school it isn't so bad.

Gregor McCallum (8)
Ayr Grammar Primary School

SNOW

I am excited
It's snow, it's snow.
I look out the window
Yes, it is here,
I jump outside,
I said, 'Snowman,'
So I made a snowman.
Scott came out next,
Scott said, 'Snowball fight?'
So we had a snowball fight,
That was OK.
I said, 'It's getting cold,
We have to go in.'
Hot chocolate to warm up.

Stuart Currie (9)
Ayr Grammar Primary School

BACK TO SCHOOL

Back to school tomorrow, oh no!
Horrible maths, awful work, oh no!
Teachers shouting, children screaming,
Playing football, oh no! Boys!
Spelling, getting told off, oh no!
Getting hurt,
Language,
Playing tig,
Falling over, oh no!
Having playtime, going to lunch,
Getting work home,
Doing homework,
School is *horrible!*

Abigail Fleming (8)
Ayr Grammar Primary School

BACK TO SCHOOL

The holidays are nearly over
It's school in two days.
Great!
I can't wait
Till Mum takes me back!
Right now my mum is in a sack,
A sack of potatoes.
Why?
But still, there are when the girls come back . . .
Boys . . . Oh no!
Still, I like my teacher!
My friends from school are;
Matthew, Gordon, Emma Lydon, David,
Emma Davis, Emma Wilson, Abigail, Nicola,
Owen and Katrina!
I love school!
When we were back to school I shouted,
Yeah, we are back!

Kathryn Dunlop (8)
Ayr Grammar Primary School

THE VIEW FROM MY BEDROOM WINDOW

Tall green conifer trees blowing in the wind.
Big brown gate closed to keep my brother in.
A medium size wall sitting nice and firm.
Flowers getting heads knocked off.
Newly mown grass blowing in the wind.

Stuart Lindsay (8)
Ayr Grammar Primary School

SNOW

I looked out the window
I saw snow and bare trees.
I said to myself,
I'll have a snowball fight
With my friends, have fun,
Make some snow angels.
I looked out again,
I saw a robin on the gatepost
An old man trudging.
I went outside and made a snowman,
I was excited.
I saw some footprints
Where do they lead?
The snow hit me cold and watery.
I went in for hot chocolate
Yum, yum.

Leanne Helm (8)
Ayr Grammar Primary School

BACK TO SCHOOL

It's nearly time to go back to school!
Teachers shouting! Spelling!
Language! Maths!
People getting shouted at!
Boys!
But I want to go back because
There is playtime, lunch time
And my favourite thing, home time!

Nicola McKinlay (8)
Ayr Grammar Primary School

THE FOREST

Sharpened creepers, creeping slowly up the trees and on the ground.
Ancient cottage, sitting, silently in a clearing, tall and wide.
Aged, ghost, floating carefully in the forest, up and around.
Blood stained knife, tumbling rapidly down the hill at the forest's side.
Golden stream, flowing aimlessly, going over the shingled ground.
Heavy, mud solidifying, insignificantly, sitting there with its
                                  muddy pride.
Light-haired, bat, fluttering spookily, a radar by sound, not light.
Stealthily, assassin, stalking mercilessly, keeping hidden, out of sight.
Terrifying scream, wailing, hopefully, and that is all.
I bid goodnight.

Louise McGaffney (10)
Ayr Grammar Primary School

THERE IS A GHOST IN MY SCHOOL

There is a ghost in my school and I hate ghosts
People play ghost tricks on me when I read Goosebumps
And if I read five pages, I freak out.
Sush, here's something,
Help, help! Don't do dark things like that on me.
One day I was walking to school,
Hello, hello, the wind blew hard against my face
Or was it the wind?
Then there was a crash,
Was it the wind or was it that ghost at school?

Axel Jorge (8)
Ayr Grammar Primary School

BACK TO SCHOOL

Oh dear! Oh no!
It's school tomorrow
I won't be able to sleep tonight.
Oh dear! Oh no!
It's school today
Better get up.
Oh dear, oh no!
We're at school
But I'll go and get a place in the line anyway
Oh dear, oh no!
We're going in.
Oh dear! Oh no!
Mad maths, rotten reading, terrible tables.
Oh good! Oh finally
School is over
But I guess it wasn't so bad!

Emma Lydon (8)
Ayr Grammar Primary School

MY SISTER

My sister is like a tree,
She grows everyday,
She has different colours of leaves.
She looks down at me.
She is wonderful.

Fiona McLean (10)
Ayr Grammar Primary School

SCHOOL

Oh no! School next week.
And it's a new class.
Will my teacher be nice?
Or will she be funny?
Will she be scary?

School, in two days! Oh no!
Well I'm back now and it's not so bad.
Well, it's not so bad at all.
Top marks from my perspective.
Stories.
Just step into one and you can do
Everything you want.
School, it's not so bad.

Silas McGilvray (8)
Ayr Grammar Primary School

MY BROTHER

A chocolate lover
A terrible brother
A homework hater
An illness faker
A football freak
An awful reek
A late sleeper
A food sneaker
A little brat
A smelly rat
A volleyball lover
Yeah! That's my brother!

Sarah Boyle (11)
Ayr Grammar Primary School

CUTE, CUDDLY AND SWEET

I looked at it
It was adorable
All that drool coming out its mouth
It looked so harmless
All that fluffy hair neatly groomed
It looked so soft and clean
Its ears were wet
From where it had been drinking
They were so long
It looks so angelic
The dog was so sweet
Its fur was so silken
I wondered what breed it was
Maybe a . . .
American spaniel or a
Springer spaniel or a
King Charles
I know a . . .
Cocker spaniel.

Lauren Campbell (10)
Ayr Grammar Primary School

BACK TO SCHOOL

The holidays are nearly over.
One week to school.
Oh no, maths, spelling, teachers shouting.
But I will see my friends.
I must remember my earplugs
For the teachers' shouting
And the bell
And school bag, pencil and rubber.

Gordon Bain (8)
Ayr Grammar Primary School

WHEN THE SNOW FALLS

When the snow falls
It's all over the walls,
And there's lots of phone calls.

When the snow falls,
The country is white,
And it is really
Quite a beautiful sight.

When the snow falls,
We all throw snow balls,
And I love it.

When the snow falls
I love it so,
Because we all
Play in the snow.

I love it.

Sisely Parks (8)
Ayr Grammar Primary School

PEACE

Peace is light blue
It smells like roses.
Peace tastes of kiwi fruit
It sounds calm and peaceful.
Peace feels soft and gentle
Peace lives in the calm heaven.

Yasmin Fleming (10)
Ayr Grammar Primary School

A SNAPPING DOG

At the door it stands,
Quite strongly on its massive hands,
In its basket it lies,
Staring at the small black flies.

Its snarling, snapping mouth starts drooling,
He thinks that he's the one ruling,
A fat chubby dog,
That sits like a hog.

He starts to fight,
With a cat that might
Just run away and hide.

The only dog that would stand and fight
In broad daylight,
On a Friday night,
Would be maybe,
You wait and see,
A terrifying rotweiller!

Julia Hannon (10)
Ayr Grammar Primary School

BIRTHDAY

Birthday is a colourful thing,
Lots of presents, brilliant things,
Mums and dads, children playing,
Children laughing, having fun.

Craig Milby (10)
Ayr Grammar Primary School

DIPSTICK MY DOG

It sits there all day and night.
He's always waiting there
Till you walk through the door.
He's cute in every way.
He is always every day.
Whenever I call him
He comes straight away
And if he's in a playful mood he plays
And cuddles you non-stop.
He always looks so loving
And you just look at him
And you fall in love with him.
He likes to go for walks
But whenever we come back
He's as scruffy as the cat.
We have to keep him clean
So that means we clean him in the bath.
After we clean him he goes to his rug
And falls straight to sleep.
That's my dog Dipstick.

Tegan Annabi (11)
Ayr Grammar Primary School

LONELINESS

Loneliness lives in prison
Where there's nothing to do
Or no one to talk too,
Loneliness is navy blue,
Loneliness sounds like someone sobbing
In their room
Loneliness feels like a thorn in your heart.

Lewis Quinn (10)
Ayr Grammar Primary School

THE WILD DOG NEXT DOOR

The dog next door is really terrifying
And everyone who goes in always comes out crying.
I wonder what it does in there
But I wouldn't like to go inside,
Even with dare.
He jumps about the garden wildly,
And when the postman comes
He tiptoes along their path quietly.
And runs away yelling help.
If he gets lost he has no fear,
Even if foxes come near.
He really loves chasing cats in the park
And wouldn't be scared if he came face to face with a shark.
His fluffy brown coat moves in the air,
And he almost bit the leg off the mayor.
The black eyes he has sparkles in the light,
But you might see him in a pitch-black night!

Scott Clark (10)
Ayr Grammar Primary School

GOLF

Golf is the colour of green,
It smells like a summer's day.
It tastes like a demented golf ball,
It sounds like a hot shot bullet,
It feels relaxing and comfortable.

Julie Farquhar (10)
Ayr Grammar Primary School

THE RAINBOW

I light up the sky with bright colours of fun,
I shine like all of the hot rays of sun,
My unusual shape, my colours so bright,
But I fade away when the day turns to night,
The end of me holds a large pot of gold,
The air that I stand in is terribly cold,
I look dazzling, fun and oh so pretty,
I cast my shadow over small town or city,
But under my coat I have no one to talk to,
To share my secrets and everyday view,
I stand proud, tall and all on my own,
Nobody visits me or gives me a phone,
Yes, sure I'm bright, my shades so colourful,
But my force can make people, oh so gullible,
They reach up high and touch me, they try,
But I just fade away into the sky,
I won't ever be seen again,
Till the rain and the sun come together again.

Amy Frew (11)
Ayr Grammar Primary School

PEACE

Violet, it's the colour of peace
It smells like blossom flowers,
It tastes like happiness,
Peace sounds like people singing,
Peace feels like lovely fruits,
It lives in Heaven.

Karis Orr (10)
Ayr Grammar Primary School

THE STORM

I am the wind, I whistle and scream,
Just like a ghost in a small child's dream,
I can destroy a house or a city,
I'll do it with ease for I have no pity.

I am the thunder when I'm angry I shout,
I'll terrify the life out of folk without a doubt,
I'll make children run screaming and crying,
From their room to the one where their parents are lying.

I am the rain and I splash in the night,
I'll flood the nations with terror and fright,
I rattle and batter against windows and doors,
I'll come in through house roofs and soak brand new floors.

I am the lightning and I'll destroy the dark night,
And I'll do it with my mighty light,
I come down to earth in forks of rage,
I am the horror of the new age.

We are the elements of the storm,
So you'd better run into the warm,
Or else we'll get you and your kin,
Cause no matter what we always win!

Michael Cunningham (11)
Ayr Grammar Primary School

COLD HEAT

On a winter's morning
The snow is crisp and white,
I pull on my clothes
For a snowball fight.

The fight begins,
Incoming snowball, I'm hit,
For this fight
You need lots of wit.

Stuart Thomson (8)
Ayr Grammar Primary School

SNOW

I woke up this morning,
I looked through the window,
I saw snow,
I felt excited,
I got ready,
I went outside,
I felt a gentle breeze,
I heard a bird singing.
It was cold,
The snow was crunchy,
All the trees were frozen,
I saw an old man trudging in the snow,
He was frowning about the weather.
I had a hot chocolate,
We made a snowman,
We were tired at the end of the day,
But that is what Christmas is all about.

Rachel McLeish (9)
Ayr Grammar Primary School

WHITE SNOW

When the snow falls
The street is white
People make snowmen
And have a snow fight.
We all have fun
Out in the snow
And while the wind gets
Ready to blow.

Inside the house
I am watching you play
You're having fun
I wish I could stay outside to play
But inside the house
I am all cosy and warm
My dinner is ready
So see you tomorrow.

Claire Wilson (8)
Ayr Grammar Primary School

FEAR

Fear is a trickle of ice down your neck.
It's a dark alley full of eyes peering at you.
Forget hope, feel fear,
Beware voices in your head.
Do not set foot in the town of fear.

Simon Stewart (10)
Ayr Grammar Primary School

A RIVER

I am as beautiful as can be,
If you look at me you will see
When tourists come there's lots of splashing,
I hate it, how they're always dashing.
I love it when children scream and shout,
All the time I gently flow
Down below me plants will grow.
With me nobody is gentle,
Sometimes I feel like just going mental!
At night I am glittery,
Or if you want, sparkly.
During the day I flow real fast
To me really the day just flies past.
Have you guessed? No never!
If you haven't . . . *I'm a river.*

Louise Young (10)
Ayr Grammar Primary School

FRIENDSHIP

Friendship is the colour of a red rose,
It smells like a tropical tree,
Friendship tastes like fruit and nuts,
It sounds like birds flying in the air,
Friendship feels relaxing and calm,
It lives in your heart.

Emma Hughes (10)
Ayr Grammar Primary School

FRIENDSHIP

Friendship is the colour blue,
It smells of strawberries,
Friendship tastes of tropical fruit,
It sounds like birds singing,
It feels soft and fluffy,
Friendship lives in your heart.

Fraser Murray (10)
Ayr Grammar Primary School

HORSES

Horses are nice and silky,
Horses smell lovely after they have been bathed,
Horses love hay,
I love horses, I am horsy mad,
Horses are nosy,
Horses live in stables.

Victoria Williams (10)
Ayr Grammar Primary School

DANCING

Dancing is the colour of all colours
It smells like white jazz shoes
It tastes like chocolate
It sounds like jazz music
It feels exciting
It lives like peace in my heart.

Shannon Donaghue (10)
Ayr Grammar Primary School

LIMP BIZKIT

Limp Bizkit is like a psycho.
He is a total nutter who never
Thinks of others.
A mental rocker.
A mad head knocker.
His hair sticks up with the help of gel.
I think he's a devil from the hottest hell.

Stuart Kirkwood (10)
Ayr Grammar Primary School

PEACE

Peace is the colour of a blue, blue sky,
It smells like fresh clean air,
Peace tastes like your favourite sweet,
It sounds like carols singing,
Peace feels like harmony,
It lives in the air.

Adam Donnan (10)
Ayr Grammar Primary School

THERE WAS A YOUNG MAN FROM DOVER

There was a young man from Dover,
Who had a nice dog called Clover,
His dog bit his nipple,
He became a cripple,
That was the man from Dover!

Craig Wallace (11)
Ayr Grammar Primary School

MY PONY RYE PYE

My chocolate pony
The owner is Tom,
He gets fed three times a day,
He loves going to shows in May,
He is 12:2hh,
The cows in the next field go moo,
Me and my pony always dress up at Hallowe'en,
The funniest thing you have ever seen,
When you ask him 'Please' he will paw the ground.
He hides his food but it is always found.

Toni Scott (11)
Ayr Grammar Primary School

AN OLD BUILDING

Ruined doors, swaying silently attached to the angry walls,
Old dog howling loudly, in a battered room,
Full boxes, opening softly, piled on the crunchy newspaper,
Spooky shadows, creeping slowly by the used-up bins,
Creepy walls, cracking angrily in the ghostly rooms,
Broken glass, shining brightly on the wooden floor,
Cold water falling heavily from the broken pipe,
But I have to remember that all this happened many years ago!

Emily Wallace (10)
Ayr Grammar Primary School

A Forgotten Hospital

Old doors creaking loudly through the echoing walls
Shattered windows glistening sharply in the moonlight
Towering walls crumbling, slowly all around
Cold wind howling noisily everywhere
Hunting moon shining brightly up in the sky
Black shapes moving swiftly through the creaking doors
Small bats flying quickly in the midnight skies
Empty rooms waiting quietly in this old building.

Lorna Mitchell (10)
Ayr Grammar Primary School

The Rainbow

I come after a storm
When it's nice and warm
I flash through the sky, my colours so bright
When the sun sends out its powerful light.
At the end of me you'll find a pot of gold,
But I'll disappear when it becomes cold.
I sit in the sky so lonely and sad
And when the sun comes out it drives me mad.
I'll disappear into the sky
Waiting for another storm to go by.

Victoria Campbell (11)
Ayr Grammar Primary School

WHEN THE SNOW FALLS

When the snow falls
People make snowmen
People are very happy
I have a lot of fun
Playing snowball fights
We sledge down hills as well.

When the snow falls
The roads are very slippy
The country is very nice
The gardens are lovely.

When the snow falls
Me and my dad always put the fire on
It feels lovely and warm
I just love it.

Nicholas Hannan (8)
Ayr Grammar Primary School

THE BOY DOWN THE STREET IS A MONSTER

The boy down the street is a monster
His feet are huge and he wears a size 15
He is enormous and gets special clothes made
He is grumpy and never has a happy face
He is mean to little children
He is a devil and comes from *Hell*!

Murray McBride (10)
Ayr Grammar Primary School

DRAGON

A flame thrower
A smoke puffer
A green scale
A leather nail
A mythical creature
A large feature
A white fang
A raging roarer
A stomping squelcher
An ember belcher
A bone cruncher
A people muncher!

Lauren Morton Macrorie (11)
Ayr Grammar Primary School

MY DOG

My dog
He barks like mad,
He's never sad,
IIe's small and mean,
Always seen,
A dog like this is very scarce,
He slavers and snarls and is very fierce.
He scratches everything in sight,
My dog's real cool, that's that all right.

Reuben McLaughlin (10)
Ayr Grammar Primary School

INSIDE THE TREASURE BOX

One day I found a treasure box
In it there were lots of jewels.
There were:
Ten glittering gold coins
Nine beautiful blue sapphires
Eight shiny sharp diamonds
Seven sparkly silver coins
Six rolling red rubies
Five gorgeous gold rings
Four fabulous pearl necklaces
Three round rusty guns
Two dangerous daggers
One marvellous treasure map and that was all.

Catriona Wright (8)
Ayr Grammar Primary School

A GENTLE DOG

My dog is kind and gentle
She has big blue eyes
That stare at me when she's laid on my lap.
She's a big dog for her age
But always in a playful mood.
She has fluffy fur that's grey and white.
I used to take her for short walks
And I knew I could always talk to her
And she would always listen.

Amber Brown (11)
Ayr Grammar Primary School

SNOW ALWAYS FALLS

When the snow falls
It is jolly and fun,
Drivers get annoyed
Because they can't get anywhere.

When the snow falls
It is very, very, very cold,
I huddle round the fire to warm up,
Sometimes we hear the Nutcracker story.

When the snow falls
I'm sometimes stuck inside,
No fun, no snowballs, no nothing.

Gemma Macleod (8)
Ayr Grammar Primary School

THE AIREDALE

The Airedale at the bottom of my street,
Has curly hair from its head to its feet,
It dances and prances around its garden,
And slavers all over (I beg your pardon),
With its teddy-like face of brown and black fur,
If my cat saw that dog it would start to purr,
Everyone loves the dog on my street,
Its cuddly and soft and ever so sweet.

Alison Jones (10)
Ayr Grammar Primary School

WHEN THE SNOW FALLS

When the snow falls
My dad calls
The snow is falling
We run out
And we run about
Throwing snowballs.

When the snow falls
The place outside is white
Some people say we might go out
And make a snowman.

I like it when the snow falls!

Rachael Dodds (8)
Ayr Grammar Primary School

A LOVELY LABRADOR

This Labrador has a silky black coat,
Has lovely brown eyes and is very stout,
He jumps about wildly and plays all day,
And goes on a picnic with his owners in May.
On rainy days he stays indoors but he is never bored,
He plays a game with his human friend,
And that game has never an end.

Alison Andrew (10)
Ayr Grammar Primary School

MY DREAM DOG

It's a fierce looking dog,
But on the inside very cute,
It's small but adorable,
But cuddly and daring,
It's a black Alsation,
A lovely caring dog,
He is different from the rest,
That is why he is my dream dog.

Blair Monaghan (11)
Ayr Grammar Primary School

MY FRIEND

My friend is like a flower,
She is the best friend to me and nature.
She's really sweet and peaceful.
Everyone agrees she is beautiful.
She grows straight and tall and
doesn't worry at all.
She wilts when she is sad.
My friend is like a flower.

Emily Fleming (10)
Ayr Grammar Primary School

A FISH

An ocean explorer
A water soarer
A fin flapper
A tail slapper
A gob gopper
A bubbling talker
A scaly dresser
A seaweed messer.

Erin Grace (11)
Ayr Grammar Primary School

MY MUM

A baby lover
A cot cuddler
An easy waker
A homework helper
A worry warrior
A cheerful cleaner!

Eleanor Parks (11)
Ayr Grammar Primary School

THE MAN FROM BERLIN

There was an old man from Berlin
Who lived in a dusty old bin
He had a dog,
Three cats and a frog
That silly old man from Berlin.

Sinead McPherson (11)
Ayr Grammar Primary School

The Young Girl Called Louise

There was a young girl called Louise
Who was totally obsessed with trees
One day in the garden
She burped and said 'Pardon'
That polite young girl called Louise.

Lara Gurun (11)
Ayr Grammar Primary School

Aliens

A   liens are ugly
L   ong ugly heads
I   n an ugly world
E   ach one is blue
N   o, I am not afraid
S   hh . . . I actually am!

Caitlin Reid (8)
Ayr Grammar Primary School

A Trip To The Moon

There was a young fellow from Troon
Who went on a trip to the moon
He took lots of food
And came back in a mood
That silly young fellow from Troon.

Aiden Jellema (11)
Ayr Grammar Primary School

LOOKING OUT MY WINDOW

Blooming in the sun
Beautiful stunning bright flowers
Swaying in the wind.

A colourful bird
Tweeting softly from a tree
In the gentle wind.

Old bumped tree trunk
Waiting, lonely to be cut down
By the man next door.

Ordinary, still pole
Holding up the washing line
In the summer sun.

Nicola Reid (11)
Ayr Grammar Primary School

ALIENS

A n alien walked up to me,
L ooking very strangely,
I t didn't move until I said,
E ither you move or you'll be dead.
N umber *ten* I said, number *nine* I said, *eight,*
S *even,* I screamed, he ran all the way down
   the hill and never was seen again.

Julie-Anne McGaffney (8)
Ayr Grammar Primary School

WHEN THE SNOW FALLS

When the snow falls . . .
When the snow falls
People make snowmen.

When it snows
The country is white.

When the snow falls
It is cosy and warm inside
And outside it is cold and frosty
But we all love it.

Samantha Hendry
Ayr Grammar Primary School

ALIENS

A liens have big glowing eyes, and big bumpy heads
L ooking down on earthlings, while we're in our beds
I   n their spaceships they float about on the planet Mars
E ating stardust cookies and all their rocket bars
N ow they're coming down to Earth from far away in Space
S o that they can study the funny human race.

Jamie O'Neil (8)
Ayr Grammar Primary School

VIEW FROM MY BEDROOM WINDOW

Brown-barked trees moving in the window,
Big reddish fences made of wood,
Red and yellow flowers that are very pretty,
Big heavy stones that are pale yellow in colour,
Large white houses with a family of four inside.

Rosie Carr (9)
Ayr Grammar Primary School

WINTER

W inter can be cold,
I ce cold hands,
N ever could be colder,
T op's freezing cold,
E xcited because Santa is coming.
R aining all over me.

Ross Dickson
Ayr Grammar Primary School

MY EYES

My eyes are green,
Green as the grass can ever be,
Green as the leaves on a palm tree,
Green as the rainforest,
Splashed with yellow,
Yellow as the bright sun,
Yellow as the lion's mane.

Eilidh Noad (8)
Ayr Grammar Primary School

MORNING

Now I don't have to get up,
We will have hard work to do,
They're always like this,
I can choose the TV show today,
I am going to the front room,
Can you get tunes?
I will feed your fish,
And we have to get to school.

David McNeil (9)
Ayr Grammar Primary School

WINTER

W ind blows strong,
I t's sad it won't last long
N ever have I seen such snow
T rees bent and swayed
E yes on presents laid
R obins dance on ice.

Jamie McFadzean (9)
Ayr Grammar Primary School

THE WINTER POEM

W indows frosted with ice,
I cicles hanging from the trees,
N o sun to be seen,
T insel on our Christmas trees,
E ars are cold and sore,
R ed squirrels trying to keep warm.

Lauren McKinstry (8)
Ayr Grammar Primary School

THE WINTER POEM

W arm and cosy I am
I feel so excited
N ow I feel cold
T he snow feels so soft
E ars, my ears are cold
R oughly I coughed.

Devon Gibson (8)
Ayr Grammar Primary School

SNOW

The old man trudges away angrily.
I am excited and happy,
I think of nice things like snowmen and Christmas,
A robin is singing and cleaning its wings.
Snow reminds me to have a snowball fight with my friend,
I feel warm in my huge jacket.
My face feels cold when the snow hits it,
I shiver and my knees knock.
I look at the trees, they are bare with no leaves,
My cottage roof is covered with snow.
The man's footsteps go *crunch, crunch,* giving me a fright,
But when it snows I am always very
       Happy!

Sarah Drain (9)
Ayr Grammar Primary School

MORNING

But I don't want to get up.
Where did my mum rush off to?
I wonder if my mum made me a drink.
I am going to get my breakfast.
Has Emma already got to the bus stop?
I wonder if Mrs Buchanan did take the train to school.
Is it time to go to school already?

Sean Adams (9)
Ayr Grammar Primary School

THIS IS OUR SUMMER PLACE

And the trees are busy with birds,
And all leaves are summer green,
And the river that we fish in
Is flowing over the stones.
The air is sweet smelling,
Our voices are loud with laughter,
And everything is warm
And playful in the summer's light.

Lissa McLeod (9)
Ayr Grammar Primary School

SUMMER SUN

This is our summer place
And all the leaves are fresh
With a touch of yellow
And the river is flowing along
Like it is a big slow helpless tortoise.
The air is like a carry balloon
And our voices are like howls
And everything is like a summer day.

Lucy Anderson (9)
Ayr Grammar Primary School

VIEW FROM OUR CLASSROOM

Grey cloudy sky threatening to rain,
Red sandstone houses empty of people,
Squawking, squabbling seagulls searching for food.
Ancient tall church spire holding a weathervane.
Glass sheltered bus stop advertising cartoon festival.

Ben Davies (9)
Ayr Grammar Primary School

THIS IS OUR SUMMER PLACE

This is our summer place
And the trees are bushy and birds are singing
And all the leaves are green and fresh
And the river is calm and gentle.
There is an amazing sight of the sea
The air is warm and clear
Our voices are smooth
And everything is loud.

Hayley Martin (9)
Ayr Grammar Primary School

EVENING

I love the evening because
I can relax and have some toast
and see the sunset.
When I go to my gran's
I do my homework and
then I go to my bed to relax.

Shaun Barrett (9)
Ayr Grammar Primary School

WINTER - WHAT I SEE

W hite snow in the garden
I   cicles frozen on the floor
N ice warm fire
T   weeting birds all around
E   veryone eating toast and drinking hot chocolate
R   obins flying around looking for shelter.

Lauren Borthwick (9)
Ayr Grammar Primary School

SNOW

I am excited about Christmas,
lots of toys,
hot chocolate to warm me up.
I see birds singing,
snowball fight with my friend, Fiona,
make angel prints in the snow,
House roof covered with snow,
Smoke curling from the chimney,
Bare trees covered in snow.

Kara McCracken (9)
Ayr Grammar Primary School

DREAM PLACE

As I looked down there were
loads of gleaming pink and purple flowers.
The sun beamed down on them
which made them sparkle and shine.

They are lovely pink and purple colours,
the colours can go down, they are like a long carpet.
The sun was beaming down and the clouds are
turning into different animals.
The place is made out of millions of little flowers.
The flowers are made out of lavender, violet, light purple
and a very dark red and a shade of pink.

Sheena Grant (11)
Clachan Primary School

HELPLESS DREAM!

On a cold and frosty morning
in mid February,
I walked to my bedroom window
and looked out. I saw the gleaming
crystal on the grass and the trees swaying from side to side.
All the cars were frosted up and cold.

After my view, I went to the kitchen
and had my breakfast, but before I did something caught my eye,
a sparkle off the frost made me want to go outside
and feel the breeze.

Just then, a gust of wind blew my long, golden hair
into my face and the wind started to
circulate with the warmth in the house.
I took one step outside and then I slipped.
I wanted to open my eyes
but I could not, because the frost had gone into them.
Just then, I had a chance, I opened them.

When I did open my eyes, I was in a dream land.
Unicorns, horses that had long white wings and could fly,
small teenagers with purple and pink flowers in their hair
to make them beautiful.
The background was gorgeous, the sea was sparkling, shimmering
and more. The trees were green and well looked after.

Just then, I stood up and blinked and then
I found myself lying on the ground
in my garden, just where I had slipped!

I was astonished. How could it have happened?
I couldn't remember a thing!

Caeliegh Kean (10)
Clachan Primary School

MIRACLES

From the edge of the cliffs I felt
as if I was on the top of the world.
No one was there.
It was just me,
on my own.
The sea thrust itself
at the bottom of the rocks.
I threw my head up and
let the wind blow my hair.
This was my place.

The great, glittering, golden sun
looked down approvingly at me.
Adrenaline rushed through
my head like a hound
after a helpless hare.
I felt like I was
going to fly and find the
road to heaven.

The gleaming, white cliffs
lay under me, full of chalk.
In the distance a ship
sailed by leaving a ripple
of water at its tail.
Golden mist
floated everywhere.
It was heaven.

I would never forget this.

Never . . .

Lisa Mears (11)
Clachan Primary School

HEAVEN IS THE PLACE TO BE

As I looked down I saw a deep, white carpet
just like the soft, sparkling snow
it seems
I had seen in another life.

I saw the specks through the curtain of lashing, watery rain.
The specks are what I thought
were my house.
I am sure I can go back there.
Or could I?
No I cannot turn back the hands of time
and go back to that angelic place.
Heaven is the place for me.
I looked up and saw the pillows of clouds
moving silently across the light blue sky.
I have moved my life on.
I am far, far away
in a place that is God's.
Now I will live forever
in a much happier place.

Fiona Mears (10)
Clachan Primary School

MY DOG

I have an old dog,
she plays in the water.
She likes to eat food
and chew bones that I bring.

I have an old cat,
she is like the dark black.
She likes to catch mice,
even though she is nice.

Daniel Richardson (10)
Craignish Primary School

SOCKS AND CLOGS

Socks is my cat
and I am very pleased about that.
A big ruff,
a load of fluff,
a ball on my bed,
a tail and a head,
and a steam engine purr.

Clogs is Tom's cat,
I'm not so pleased about that.
A small ruff,
a massive amount of fluff,
a ball on Tom's bed,
a tail and a head,
and a tremendously loud purr.

Two extremely pretty cats in our house!

Isla Graham (10)
Craignish Primary School

TIME

Time is nothing, but something,
Time is there, but it's not.
Time is huge, but so small.
You can't stop time,
Or freeze it.
Time is there, but it's not.
Time goes by really fast, but slow.
Time makes things change very quickly.
Time is old and time is new.
It takes time to do anything.
Time is old and time is new.
Time grows, but time shrinks.
Time is there, but it's not.
You can only see time if it's on a clock.

Chloe Potter-Irwin (9)
Craignish Primary School

BAR-BABY

Bar-Baby has lots of spots.
Some of her spots are big,
Some of her spots are small.
She has grey on her,
She has a small black tail.
She has a black mane.
Sometimes she is good,
Sometimes she is bad.

Cara Campbell (9)
Craignish Primary School

THE EVACUEE

I've just came off the train,
I'm missing ma mammy
I've got ma wee bonnet on
And I've got ma gas mask box roon ma neck.
I've got ma woolly scarf wrapped roon me tae.
I am wearing ma big, cosy jacket.
I'm going to live in a new hoose wi' a woman called Maria
And her son called Jocky.
It's been a long day for me.

The town was a lovely sight,
I'm in the hoose,
It's a lovely big hoose.
The people are really nice.
I'm in ma pyjamas and I'm ready to go to sleep.

Alyson Gillies (11)
Dalintober Primary School

ON THE STAGE

O n the stage is the scariest part of all,
N erves let me down when I try to sing.

T ry not to look at your friends or you'll be embarrassed,
H ave a good time, it's the only way,
E ven if you are scared to death.

S o now the show is about to end,
T he crowd goes wild with lots of joy
A nd bet of all, they think we're . . .
G reat!
E vening's now over and they think it's a super show.

Greg Gillespie (11)
Dalintober Primary School

MY CHRISTMAS PREPARATIONS

Christmas comes but once a year
And it's a very joyous time,
With things like presents and parties.
It makes everybody's spirits high.

I wish Christmas was every day,
With decorations, lights and a tree,
There's also carol singing and shows,
Too bad it's not for free.

It's the last day and the suspense is killing,
I've put up the stocking and the cake's fulfilling,
With my snack for Santa and Rudolf fed,
I think it's time to go to bed.

Scott McGeachy (11)
Dalintober Primary School

EXCUSES

The dishes are clean enough
And anyway, it's not my turn, so tough!
I'm too much of a busy bee
And I've got company.

I'm allergic to the water,
Also, it keeps getting hotter.
The tap won't turn,
It's too hot, I'll get a burn.

I'm going out, to the Dome,
I've been eaten by a giant gnome.
I'm feeling sick,
I'm too busy in the nick.

Catherine Strang (11)
Dalintober Primary School

THE EVACUEE

I'm nearly there,
There's no more smoke,
It's very peaceful in the country.
I don't know what do,
I wonder where I'll go?
What will happen to me?
Will they like me, will they hate me?
I don't know what I'll do.
Where are they taking me now?
I miss my mum already.
Only one day, hasn't yet passed,
It seems like years and years,
But not one day has passed.

Ruaridh McAulay (11)
Dalintober Primary School

THE EVACUEE

She came like a package to the door,
Didn't know where she was anymore,
Knocking and knocking hard as she could,
I think she was in an upset mood.
She had left her parents at Waterloo,
She didn't really know what to do.
Her mother was needed in the field,
Her father was injured with wounds to be healed.
Her mother's name was Mairi,
Her father's name was Harry,
And the evacuee was Carrie.

Katie Wallace (11)
Dalintober Primary School

I WAS LATE FOR SCHOOL BECAUSE

I was late for school because
I slept in.
I was late for school because
I fell in a puddle.
I was late for school because
My dog wouldn't let me out.
I was late for school because
I had to finish my homework.
I was late for school because
My dog died.
I was late for school because
My mum ate my homework.
I was late for school because
A dog ate my finger.
I was late for school because
I had to go to the vet.
I was late for school because
Mrs Glendinning ran me over.
I was late for school because
An alien landed in my garden and
Ate my big brother.

Craig Anderson (11)
Dalintober Primary School

MY CHRISTMAS PREPARATIONS

Christmas isn't far away,
I am going crazy.
I wish it was tomorrow,
Otherwise I'll be in sorrow.

In the school there's Christmas Post,
I did it the other day.
When you're doing it, it's really fun,
My Christmas presents will weigh a ton.

I'd better get Santa's beer and cake,
And carrots for Rudolf too.
It's time to put up the Christmas tree
And then it's bed for me.

Darren Anderson (11)
Dalintober Primary School

THE EVACUEE

I am leaving the city
On the big train
Saying goodbye to my friends,
Leaving my mum.
The Germans are coming,
They'll bomb everything
And people will die.

My suitcase is packed
With my personal stuff.
I feel lonely and tired
Hoping the new people will like me.
What will I do if they don't?

The train is steaming
And they're waiting for us to get on.
I have a packed lunch with egg sandwiches
And some fresh water.

I'm hoping that I'll be back soon
When I can meet my friends and
Talk about what they did.
On the train, I'll sit at the window
And I'll try to be happy.

Laura-Jane McCallum (11)
Dalintober Primary School

OUR SCHOOL SHOW

It's time to go.
My legs were shaking,
So were my toes,
But I was OK.

We made our way down to the hall,
Giggling and laughing,
Trying not to fall,
so that was OK.

The snapping of fingers begins,
Clicking and clapping,
We all had some fun,
That was great.

The second song had been sung,
We all knew what it was time for,
It was time for some fun,
It was great.

We finished the songs and
Made our way off,
Dancing and prancing,
Cough, cough, cough!

The night was over,
We all had a laugh
And everyone's in clover,
It was enjoyed by all.

Seona McNaughton (11)
Dalintober Primary School

OUR SCHOOL SHOW

It's time to go
And have a laugh,
I'm so nervous, I can't stand the blast!
I just can't help it,
I'll let my nerves go free.

Can't I just stop
Being so excited,
I'll try and calm down,
But I'm far too ecstatic.
I'll do my best to keep on going,
It's kind of hard
When you're dancing the night away!
I gradually calm down
Before we go on stage.

It's not long to go,
Until it's P7's turn.
Then I feel so unhappy,
I can't believe it,
It's Primary Seven's very last turn.
We won't be doing any more shows.
I'll try and be jolly,
But that will not work.
What shall I do?

Hannah Colville (11)
Dalintober Primary School

CHRISTMAS PREPARATIONS

Christmas is coming,
It's fast approaching.
Shows have begun,
The stage is exploding.
Calendars are up
On the first of December.
Five, four, three, two, one.
Trees are towering over everyone,
This great occasion has just begun.
On the night before Christmas,
We leave out a sack
For when Santa drops in
To fill up our sacks.
Stockings are held above the chimney,
Waiting to get filled with sweets and treats.
It's nearing the day,
It's nearing Christmas.

Andrew Lazarus (11)
Dalintober Primary School

OUR SCHOOL SHOW

Our school's getting dressed up
'Cause the show's on the way!
I'm very, very excited.
Only a week today,
Everyone's getting ready.
Rehearsals every day.
Our show's called 'West Side Story'
It's a good play.

Everyone has cool costumes,
Including me too.
When the show is over,
I'll be saying 'Phew!'
I've seen all the acts
But my favourite must be
Little Winnie the Pooh.
What a pleasure to see!

Kelly Brodrick (11)
Dalintober Primary School

I WAS LATE FOR SCHOOL BECAUSE . . .

I was late for school because
I slept in.
I was late for school because
My bike was broken.
I was late for school because
The car wouldn't start.
I was late for school because
Walking from my house takes 15 minutes!
I was late for school because
My wee sister was ill.
I was late for school because
My mum was in the bathroom, and she takes ages!
I was late for school because
I forgot to put my trainers on.
I was late for school because
On the way to school, I was kidnapped by Martians
And I was taken to Mars.
Luckily, Superman saved me.

Colin Millar (11)
Dalintober Primary School

I WAS LATE FOR SCHOOL BECAUSE . . .

I was late for school because
I slept in.
I was late for school because
The cat was sick on me.
I was late for school because
I thought it was a school holiday.
I was late for school because
I forgot to do the lines you gave me,
So I had to do them this morning.
I was late for school because
My gerbil died.
I was late for school because
Dad wanted me to eat.
I was late for school because
I was visiting Robbie Williams!
I was late for school because
I broke my leg.
I was late for school because
I went to Africa.
I was late for school because
My brother gave me a bomb
And it took *ages* to eat it.
I was late for school because
There was an avalanche and
It landed on our house!
I was late for school because
A sabretooth tiger ate my big sister
And I've been celebrating!
I was late for school because
I was busy watching Ruth and Jamie kissing.
I was late for school because,
Oh, what's the use, you won't believe me anyway!

Katie Conley (11)
Dalintober Primary School

CHRISTMAS PREPARATIONS

We are starting to get into the festive mood
As we are into December.
Out buying cards and advent calendars
Shopping for presents and decorations.

As we start to get ready for our Christmas show,
Practising our singing and hymns for church,
We start to help Mum put decorations up,
The baubles on the tree and the candles.

We go to the parties and eat the food
And do all the last of the shopping.
It's Christmas Eve and we're all excited
Leaving our stockings and snack for Santa.

Jennifer McMillan (11)
Dalintober Primary School

NERVES

My knees are watery,
Enough to smash the crockery.
West Side Story is our show,
You might, maybe know.
Shaking, quaking, nerves,
They're kicking in like tennis serves.

Lights, camera, action,
That's what we've got, maybe a fraction.
My stomach's like a can of jumping beans,
I'm going to be sick over these jeans.

Now the day has passed,
It went so fast.

Andrew Henderson (11)
Dalintober Primary School

MY CHRISTMAS PREPARATIONS

Christmas is coming,
Christmas goes pop!
Putting up the tree makes me want to hop.
Christmas decorations,
Baubles on string,
The Christmas carollers are getting ready to sing.
I wonder what I'll get for my mum and dad.
If I don't get them anything, they'll be very sad.
Christmas dinner . . . yummy, yummy, yummy,
When my sister sees it, she will not be asking for a dummy.
Writing all the Christmas cards is such fun,
When you hear the crackers run, run, run.
Christmas is my favourite time of year,
I can't wait till Christmas is here.

Claire McFadzean (10)
Dalintober Primary School

MY CHRISTMAS PREPARATIONS

I open the window of my advent calendar
I get a little surprise when I do.

In school we do our Christmas plays
In church the children do a nativity play.

I help put up the Christmas tree,
I put up the decorations as well.

On Christmas Eve we leave a snack for Santa,
We put all our presents on a seat each.

Matthew Turner (11)
Dalintober Primary School

BYE-BYE, MA

Me and me pal were at the station
Wi' oor box hanging fae oor necks.
The teachers called oor names and
Shoved us on the train.

I called to me ma,
'I'll miss you, I'll miss you.'
I dinna ken if we'll meet again,
So I said me last words,
'I love you.'

The tears were streaming doon me face
And a' the bairns were greeting tae.
I dinna ken if I'll be happy again.

Cheryl Brown (11)
Dalintober Primary School

THE SEASIDE

The sea is cold
The sea is wavy
The sea is wild
The sea is stingy
I like the sea
Because you can water-ski
Sailing is fun
Bumping up and down on the wavy sea
I love the banana boat
Because you fall off
When you go to the sea have as much fun as me.

Fiona Douglas (9)
Forehill Primary School

MY SCOOTER

How I love my scooter, lovely as can be,
On December 25th, it just came to me.
It came in blue paper, which was diamond shiny,
Whizzing down the street, I swear I did about ninety.

It has two blue wheels.
Oh, how lovely it feels
To zoom ahead down Cloverhill,
With joy each day I am filled.

I love my scooter, I do, I do.
On December 25th, Malcolm got one too.
We went for him, my brother and me,
Which made our gang to a total of three.

I'm best friends now with my one of these things
Which rule over cars.
I'll maybe some day go to Mars,
And if I do, those shiny silver bars
Will come with me too!

Jamie Edgar (11)
Forehill Primary School

CHOCOLATE

It's tasty and it's creamy,
But sometimes a bit big and beany.
It's lovely and it's melted,
As long as it's kept hot and sheltered.
Sometimes nice, sometimes not . . .
But I'll give anything chocolatey a shot.
It's nice and gooey, sometimes chewy,
And always in the shop shouting, 'Cooeee.'

Oh how I love it so much,
It's nice and soft to my touch.
If I had to part with it,
I'd probably jump into a pit.
I'd sit down in a deep, dark den,
And never come out to the Earth again,
Hide away from the big, bad world,
Without my beloved *chocolate!*

Kirsty Mackie (11)
Forehill Primary School

MY DARTBOARD

My dartboard looks the best,
Definitely better than the rest.
Black and blue with a little red and white
You could say it's a lovely sight.

I wonder how my dartboard feels,
I bet it wishes it has some wheels
To race around in my room,
Instead of spending all day filled with gloom.

Oh, the pain
When the dart hits its circular heart.
You hear a noise as if it's going to fall apart.
We are like bread and butter.
When it comes to playing darts,
I'm a nutter.

Darren Swan (11)
Forehill Primary School

SPACE

Space is giant,
It's also very silent.
Venus, Mercury and Mars
Always will float beside a big star.

Earth is the only place
With water upon its face,
But you won't have fun
If you happen to land on the Sun.

I shall flee
When I see the giant Saturn V
Getting wheeled to the pad by the crawler,
As I walk in my spacesuit fastening my collar.

I wish I could see the moon and stars,
Maybe even land on Mars.
I love space,
It's a great place.

Neil Stoddart (11)
Forehill Primary School

TAKE-OFF!

In class I dream of flying in a shuttle,
But then Mrs Shanta wakes me with a cuddle.
I think of spreading my wings and flying away,
Oh man, that would be a wonderful day!
The spaceship would take off with a mighty blast,
And I think that I must be going super fast.

As the gravity disappears,
I let go of all my fears.
After five minutes I feel a sudden jolt
And think, 'Was that my fault?'
I look out of the window, oh what a sight!
An asteroid flew by and gave me an awful fright.
I woke up on my desk with a sore shoulder
And thought, 'Maybe . . . when I'm older.'

Ross Clarkson (11)
Forehill Primary School

TOYS

There they stand, the soldier army,
With bouncy balls, going barmy.
Robots buzzing, shooting their lasers,
Teddies sitting being lazy.
Yo-yos bobbing up and down
Electronic dogs giving a frown.

Barbies singing,
Games a-playing,
Lego falling to the ground.
Whoopee cushions making rather a rude sound,
Cars flying round tight corners,
Pictures waiting to be coloured,
Forgotten things in your cupboard.
Toys are brilliant for having fun,
Be sure to share them with everyone.

Craig MacMorland (11)
Forehill Primary School

BEANIE BABIES

Chocolate Moose has orange anglers,
His only dream is for sweets to glide
Through is own little world.
Sherbet, sugar he likes to eat,
But can you guess his favourite sweet?

Early Robin's voice is neat,
Other birds just seem to chitter and tweet.
On television she is, every week,
Famous artists for her they seek.
Singing is a great profession,
Sign up now for an hour's lesson!

Whisper Deer is quiet and small,
Compare her to anyone they'll be towering tall.
So beautiful her beady black eyes are,
Dark as the night sky so far,
Though only a fawn, she's tough inside.

Bushy Lion won't roar - he'll purr instead,
So always pat him on the head.
A cuddly kitten he'll promise to be,
Warm and soft - he wouldn't hurt a flea.
Long, powerful legs, lightning quick,
He'll be there if you're in a stick.

So with Bushy, Early, Whisper, Chocolate and all,
Collect every one, you'll have a ball!

Emma Cairns (11)
Forehill Primary School

THE MILLENNIUM PARTY

Whizz, fizz, flash and pop!
My mum runs around the busy shop.
She grabs everything she can,
She found the last lonely apple.
She bought the first big jar of jam.

Whizz, fizz, flash and pop!
My mum screams, 'Hurry up!' and 'Chop, chop!'
We put up fancy decorations,
Balloons, party poppers, streamers too,
But we cannot find those invitations.

Whizz, fizz, flash and pop!
My mum hands me a sopping, soapy mop.
She asked me to clean the bathroom,
Then told me to use a thing called a vacuum.

Whizz, fizz, flash and pop!
The ball is just about to drop.
The music is loud,
Soul, Indie and lots of pop.
Everyone cheering 'Happy New Year,'
Oh what a crowd!

Whizz, fizz, flash and pop!
The music's gone and I'm ready to flop.
I went to bed after a giant yawn,
My mum woke me up with the whistle of a cop
And told me I went to bed at the crack of dawn.

Stewart McKie (11)
Forehill Primary School

IN THE CITY

Houses in the city are very tall,
But none as tall as the shopping mall.
The shopping mall with hundreds inside,
To find your way you need a tour guide.
A mum with bags, her child horribly nags,
Families in a care, to spend their day.
Mum goes in Mackays,
In there a dress she buys,
We walk down the stairs to C & A,
I choose a skirt and go to pay.
Out of there into the Guide's Shop
Where I choose a colourful yellow top,
That's enough of the city for one day,
I'll be back on Saturday.

Aya Musbahi (11)
Forehill Primary School

CITY LIFE

Buildings, towers and offices - they're all so tall,
In fact, I'm sure hardly any are small.
Taxis, buses and cars - the traffic is mad!
People in jams just despair and are sad,
But here's the more positive side to life in the city,
For not all of it is misery and pity.
You can trot to the shops for a blether,
Take your car depending on the weather.
The city at night is full of bright light,
Ruby red, ocean blue, emerald green and cloud white.
It really is the most wonderful sight.

Rachel Anderson (11)
Forehill Primary School

THE CENTRUM ARENA

I love to go skating five days a week
The Centrum in Prestwick is where I go.
Whatever the weather, summer or bleak,
On my two days off, I miss it though.

Walking through the doors, the feeling is nice,
The Centrum makes me smile and I feel happy.
I walk in and I can tell when Alec cuts the ice,
Our warm-up is like old ladies yapping.

When the session is finished, my cheeks are ruby red,
Next we do our stretch-off, which is good for me,
Now all I dream of is going to my nice, warm bed
Yum! I will go home for my tea.

I sometimes go at six in the morning,
There are sessions, classes or maybe advice.
I'm up skating when most of my class are yawning.

Fiona Rosamond (11)
Forehill Primary School

THE SEA

The sea is calm.
The sea is cool.
I think about it when I'm at school.
The waves are sometimes very small,
But they might be big and tall.
Sometimes I think they are very cool.
I like the sea very much,
It makes me feel very happy.

Elaine Stoddart (9)
Forehill Primary School

WILLY, THE WEEPING WILLOW

There he sits alone in the park,
24-7, light or dark.
Little children pulling at his rough brown bark,
He sighs to himself and says, 'Oh, what a lark!'

There he sits alone all through the day
From the 1st of June to the 31st of May.
Dogs and cats jump at him happy and gay,
He sighs to himself and says, 'Oh how I wish that I could play!'

There he sits alone all through the night,
He looks ahead but no one's in his sight.
He wraps his skinny branches around his trunk so tight,
He sighs to himself and says, 'Oh I wish it could be light!'

There he sits alone giving up hope,
A little girl comes along with a skipping rope.
'Do you want to play tree? Please don't say nope!'
The tree smiles to himself and says, 'I think I can cope.'

There he sits with all his friends in the park,
His days are always bright and his nights are never dark.
Little children read to him and scribble on his bark,
He giggles to himself and says, 'Life's just a lark.'

Nicola Leonard (11)
Forehill Primary School

MY BROTHER

I have an annoying brother,
I wish I could swap him for another.
He used to always swear,
He used to have no hair.

I have an annoying brother,
I wish I could swap him for another.
Now he will never swear,
And now he has some hair.

Kevin McHarg (10)
Forehill Primary School

SPACE

Mercury is first, closest to the sun,
I wonder if it ever has any fun?

Next it's Venus, the planet of love,
A lovely rocky planet that shimmers in the sun.

Earth is the planet which we all live on,
Yes, you've guessed it - it's my favourite one!

The red planet is next, that's Mars
My favourite chocolates are . . . bars.

Jupiter is the biggest planet of all.
I hope it's not too heavy or it might fall.

Saturn is a lovely, icy planet.
Swish, swish, swish as the rings go by.

Uranus with its green and blue colour,
Like grass in a river.

Neptune is second to last,
The sun can hardly get past.

Pluto is the darkest, coldest planet,
I certainly wouldn't want to go.

I love space.

Stephanie Leske (11)
Forehill Primary School

SPACE

I simply love space,
I really like looking at the moon's face.
It's shaped like a penny
Except made of so many.

Constellations, planets and stars,
Uranus, Venus, the Sun and Mars.
There are so many space stations
From so many nations.

Far, far away, gleaming rockets
Look as if they could fit in my pockets.
I'm hoping to go to space some day,
It certainly won't be today.

Darren McCann (11)
Forehill Primary School

MY BED

When I come home from school at night
You hold out your hands waiting for me
I come bouncing and jumping up to you,
You're my wonderful bed!

You feel so snug and warm
Covering me up with your long, soothing cover.
Oh what a spectacular, sensational feeling,
You're my wonderful bed!

When sitting in class I dream of you,
Your gleaming colours and your carved wooden stands.
Oh how I wish that school would just stop
And I could go home to my wonderful bed!

Ian Chapman (11)
Forehill Primary School

MY BED

My bed is long and tall,
It stands against a lime and purple wall.
It has a built-in sofa too,
I watch TV from it and have a brilliant view.
It also has a desk
Which I love the best.
I do my homework at this
And the peace and quiet is bliss.

When I climb into my bed at night,
I feel so warm and tight.
When I have a dream,
I feel like I'm swirling in ice cream.

Sarah Sargent (11)
Forehill Primary School

MY DOGS

Long, soft, silky coats,
Their heads in a bowl like a castle in a moat,
They love to run in a wide open space,
They can run so fast they'd *never* lose a race!
Sitting longingly for their food,
They're good friends to have, *never* cheeky or rude!
With their warm, glowing, chestnut eyes,
It would melt *any* heart of stone!
Settling down in their warm, cosy blanket,
As good as gold,

Until the mischief starts!

Stephanie Britt (11)
Forehill Primary School

My Trip To The Sea

My family and I went to the beach
To have a swim in the sea.
The sun was shining on me.
I thought the water was absolutely freezing,
I came out as I was wheezing.
Later I decided to go water-skiing
But the water was so choppy I fell off my water-skis.
So I went and got my banana float,
My little brother got his rubber boat.
My nana, papa and mum were lying on the beach snoring.
I thought that was pretty boring.
A little later, I walked into the sea
Until it was up to my knee.
The sun was still beaming
When I ran out screaming
Away from the freezing cold sea.
Soon it was time for dinner and I got fish on a Chinese dish.
Later I decided to go and look at the starfish and other kinds of fish.
What a day!

Rachel McCutcheon (9)
Forehill Primary School

My Best Friend

It was on a nice summer's day
On the twentieth of May,
I went for my best friend
O that was a day I wished would never end.

We went down the river to fish
Then afterwards had a lovely dish
With fish and chips and chicken too,
'Oh no, it's too much, I'm going to spew.'

After a nice, cool refreshing drink,
We hoped like bunnies to the nearest sink.
Our hands were filthy with bits of dirt,
Oh wash off or else, I'll have to wear a skirt.

It was getting dark
And we decided to go back
To our nice warm homes
And listen to the Rolling Stones.

Craig Maxwell (11)
Forehill Primary School

THE SEA

Find a space in the beach then put up your parasol.
Get changed and grab your ball.
Run into the *sea*!
Toss the ball to your friend.
Soak your friend and they'll soak you!
Build sandcastles and watch the sea knock them down.
Jump in the sea, splash in the sea, do anything in the sea.
Go and get ice cream and then splash in the sea.
Go snorkelling or scuba diving (if you get the chance).
Watch all the birds flying over you.
Play fetch with your dog.
Swim until the water touches your chin.
When you're wet you can cover yourself in sand.
You can do lots of things in the sea.
I love it!

Melissa Brown (9)
Forehill Primary School

WALK THE DOG NOW!

Mums say
Walk the dog -
I'm playing on the PlayStation.

For the second time
Walk the dog
I've got the bad guy!

For the third time
Walk the dog.
I can't go right now!

For the *last* time
Walk the dog now!
Not long, nearly there now.

Do you even know what
I've been saying for the
Last half hour?
No, what?
Never mind, I'll
Walk the dog
Myself!

Isla McCreath (11)
Forehill Primary School

IF I WAS HOME ALONE

With my family away to Canada
I can do what I want for weeks,
But only one thing, my bird is still here.

I can eat lots of chocolate bars,
I can buy lots of jokes to play on people,
I can have my friends over without permission.

I can play my brother's computers with my bird,
I can eat fish and chips whenever I want to,
I can watch TV every day.

I can stay up all night,
I can have lots of midnight feasts,
I can go to Laser Land.

Martin Clifford (10)
Forehill Primary School

MY MUM

My mum can sometimes be really kind to me,
But sometimes can be as annoying as can be.
She really tries her best,
To put you to the test.
She sometimes thinks she's so rough,
I sometimes find it really tough!

Tidy your room are the words said to me,
Why should I? Leave me bc.
My dad comes in,
The first thing I say,
Is, 'Can I go out to play?'

I come back in and run upstairs,
Tidy my room and go downstairs.
My dad says, 'I'll go and check her room,'
It's as tidy as a silver spoon!

No it's not! My mum checks for herself.
So it is!
When did you tidy?
I have my time
That's my mum, she tries to stay fine!

Laura McGrath (11)
Forehill Primary School

MOJO BONES

This story starts in Florida,
The perfect place to be,
Downtown Disney in the Rainforest Cafe,
The waitress took our order,
And my uncle Tom said,
'I'll have the mojo bones,
With a side portion of bread.'

We all fell to the floor,
Laughing on the ground,
Because when they came they must
Have weighed a pound.

When he came to my house,
Me and my cousin said,

'I'll have the mojo bones,
With a side portion of bread!'

Scott Clark (11)
Forehill Primary School

MY GRAN!

My gran is the best gran
even though she's crazy about bran.
She rides a motorbike in a place far away
she told me she could ride one every day.

I get so excited when she's coming to tea
I tidy my room and shout with glee.
My gran would rather sit on a surfboard than a chair
she has got lovely, brown fuzzy hair.

She writes songs and plays them on her guitar
she rides about in a funky car.
Her eyes are a deep, deep blue,
I can tell you that this poem is true!

Kate Husband (11)
Forehill Primary School

MY DOG DID A PIDDLE

My dog did a piddle
Right up the vertical blinds
And all he did was smile.

My dog got a right kicking
He ran into his cage
And all he did was smile.

My dog bit my hand
It started to bleed
And all he did was smile.

My dog stole my dinner
I was hungry
And all he did was smile.

My dog ate a spider
It was still alive
And all he did was smile.

My dog did a brown accident on the floor
And my dad had to clean it up
And all he did was smile.

PS: My dog is a big pain.

Alistair Muirhead (10)
Forehill Primary School

MY BIG BROTHER IS A PAIN

My big brother is a big pain
He hits me and shouts at me
So I run upstairs to tell Mum.

My big brother is a big pain
Because he is a crabby chops
He is sometimes.

My big brother is the best in the world
But I have got to tell you
Sometimes I start the argument
And he finishes it.

But I love him very much.

Kerrie Rae (10)
Forehill Primary School

THE LITTLE FISH

I'm a little fish,
People think I'd make
A good dish!
Fish and chips for me
One day.
But I just wish they'd
Go away.
'Ummmm fish,' they say
'I'll eat you,' they say
But all I've got to say is
'I'll try not to be caught one day.'

Stephanie Coughtrie (9)
Forehill Primary School

LISTEN UP

Hi, everyone listen up,
I'm having a party,
We're going to the movies,
I'm only allowed five people,
Which people will I choose?

I'll choose Jamie because he's very brainy and
He'll tell us what the movie's all about.
I'll choose Ben because he's my friend and
He'll be kind and share.
I'll choose Jack that's a fact because he goes
To the movies every day.
I'll choose Granny because she's never out,
Always stuck inside the house.

And the last person is me because it's my party
And I'm all these things.

Lee Anderson (10)
Forehill Primary School

THE SEA

As I sail upon the choppy sea
The wind blows along with me.
The waves are high, the waves are low,
Fishes pounce and bounce along,
And shells and cockles are collected.
While sandcastles are being made,
The sea is calm, still and cold.
The sun is shining,
And ice creams have been sold.

Mairead McCrossan (9)
Forehill Primary School

MY GRANDAD

My grandad is a lunatic!
And is stronger than my dad.
He's always cracking jokes
That are really, really bad.

He even wants to wrestle me!
But I can't get around,
That tubby, muscley body,
That is lying on the ground.

He helped me when I was very young,
And now it's my turn,
To help him out and never shout,
And to help him now he's old!

Daniel Walsh (11)
Forehill Primary School

FISHES

The sea holds many different kinds of fish
And many kinds of pearls too.
There's also the master of the sea:
The great white shark.
He bosses all wee fish
And gobbles them up.
But there was one little fish
Who said, 'Can't catch me in the
Deep, deep, choppy blue sea.'

Lacie McKenna (9)
Forehill Primary School

MONSTERS

Monsters, monsters everywhere,
big and scary with lots of hair,
they eat lots and lots of gruesome food,
but you don't see them in a mood.

They sit in a cave all day and night,
you don't want to see them put up a fight,
their feet are big and smelly,
and they don't have a telly.

It must be boring living like that,
as I would be out playing with a bat,
I love it just staying as me,
going out and being free.

Lauren Clancy (10)
Forehill Primary School

MY PET

I've got a pet
who sleeps in my bed.
All day long
he licks me with his tongue.

When he is outside
he's always in a fight.
When he is in a mood
he won't get his food.

When we are at the beach
it's fun when he eats a peach.
What would I do if I never had a pet?
I would sleep all day long in my bed.

Jeffrey Van Der Sluis (10)
Forehill Primary School

THE DAY MY LITTLE PUPPY CAME HOME

The day my little puppy
came home, that's the day
I'll never forget.

His sweet and cute and
furry face made me
cry in happiness.

We were thinking of a
name for him, I thought
something beginning with T.

Then I thought Tam, but Tim
for short, but my mum said
it did not make sense.

After a while we thought of a name
that was Timmy, but
Tim for short.

Timmy, Timmy, that's his name
get up to mischief
but always gets framed!

He sits at the top of my chair
and barks out the
window if anyone's there.

But I love him so, so much
and that is my little sweet
puppy Tim.

Kirsten Little (11)
Forehill Primary School

TEACHERS I HAVE HAD AT FOREHILL PRIMARY

In primary 1 my teacher was Mrs Hayes.
She was very funny.
She was very kind and nice.
She always made you happy whenever you were sad.

In primary 2 my teacher was Mrs Lynsay.
She was very funny.
She was there whenever you may need her.
She always made you welcome.

In primary 3 my teacher was Mrs Douglas.
She was very funny.
She was very happy.
She was very polite.

In primary 4 my teacher was Mrs Johnston.
She was very funny.
She was very good at art.
She was very good at drawing.

In primary 5 my teacher was Mrs Samson.
She was very funny.
She was very nice.
She was very kind.

Now I am in primary 6 I have got Mrs Brown.
She is very funny.
She is mallow mad.
She is very helpful.

All of my teachers are very nice.

Lisa Cumming (10)
Forehill Primary School

My Torturing Maths Teacher!

My maths teacher is Mrs Brown
who always flings fractions at us
I like them, they're easy, but some people don't

My maths teacher is funny and cool
but when it's maths she's down to business
no funny business here

My maths teacher is my class teacher
she shouts a lot and gives ticks a lot
but is still very cool!

My maths teacher gives us too much homework
now we're on percentages (it's really hard)
I love tenths and fractions too

When you get in trouble
she roars like a lion
stings like a bee

But most of all
I love maths.

Laura Jamieson (10)
Forehill Primary School

The Feel Of Things

I like the feel of soft, squashy Beanie Babies all over my body.
I like the feel of sloppy, gooey wet sand on my bare feet.
I like the feel of a hard, smooth PlayStation controller on my hands.
I like the feel of a soft, cuddly puppy in my hands.
I like the feel of bubbly, silky chocolate melting.

I don't like the feel of a spiky pineapple poking at my fingers.
I don't like the feel of sticky jam sticking to my fingers.
I don't like the feel of my wibbly, wobbly ear lobe swinging to and fro.
I hate the feel of slimy worms sliding up my arm.
I don't like the feel of bumpy, lumpy trees rubbing against my hand.

Scott McEwan (8)
Forehill Primary School

MY FAMILY

In my family -

My brother is a little young.
He is quite funny.
My brother did an accident in my mum's
Arm, of course it was nice and squidgy.

In my family -

My sister is annoying.
She is kind but annoying.
She likes me but she's annoying,
That's because she's a girl.

In my family -

My mum is the oldest.
My mum is quite cool
But she likes my brother the best.

In my family -

My dad is younger than my mum.
My dad is cool.
My dad is the best of all.

David Marshall (10)
Forehill Primary School

IF I WAS HEAD . . .

If I was head . . .
Everyone would still be in bed!
We'd arrive here at one
And then just have fun!
If I was head . . .

If I was head . . .
The pencils would not be made of lead,
They would be made of Flumps!
And the paper would be custard (without any lumps).
If I was head . . .

If I was head . . .
Teachers would be banned
And I'm sure they'd understand
If I painted the loo lime,
(To match all the slime).
If I was head . . .

Just one more thing,
I think it would be cool
If I was head,
There would be no school!

Claire McNaught (10)
Forehill Primary School

THE FEEL OF THINGS

I like the feeling of my dog's soft, fluffy, smooth fur.
I like the feeling of a hard pencil in my hand.
I like the feeling of rubber, soft, smooth, squashy and wobbly.
I like the feeling of bark, rough and hard.
I like the feeling of my silky, furry jumper.

I don't like the feel of slimy, gooey gunge in my hand.
I don't like the feel of rough, jagged Velcro rubbing against my arm.
I don't like the feel of cold, hard metal in my hand.
I don't like the feel of wet, gooey, sloppy sand sticking to my feet.
I don't like the feel of squashy, slippy, slimy slugs that slide
                                        along the ground.

Colin Forbes (8)
Forehill Primary School

THINGS I LOVE TO DO TO MY SISTERS

I'll have to start by saying
I love to push and pull
My little sister Claire
At the deep end of the pool.

Then I start to annoy her
As usual that's what I do,
The only time I don't
Is when she's in the loo.

Now we come to Cheryl,
She's the bugging one,
Sometimes I want to buy her
A poisonous hot cross bun.

Sometimes when she hits me
I get really mad,
But Mum does not talk to her
She hits me and says I'm bad.

Stephen Simpson (10)
Forehill Primary School

WILD ANIMALS

I had a bull in school,
It was really a fool,
It rampages at my teacher,
It does worse to my headteacher.

I had a lion at school,
It roars in the pool,
It jumps on the tables,
It eats up all the birds.

I had a giraffe in school,
It had a neck the size of my school,
It stamps on all of the children,
It burps and blows everyone away.

I had an elephant in school,
It sucks up all the pool,
It picks up children with its ears,
It fell through the top floor to the bottom.

Kieran Todd (10)
Forehill Primary School

THE FEEL OF THINGS

I don't like slimy, squashy beetles creeping across my leg.
I don't like squashy, gooey slugs slithering over leaves.
I don't like tickly, silent ants creeping up my knees.
I don't like gooey, sloppy, wet sand sticking to my feet.
I don't like slimy, squashy soap slipping down my tummy.

Ryan Todd (8)
Forehill Primary School

MY BROTHER

My brother is a pain
When friends come round,
We try in vain
To just keep him out.

My brother is a pest
When it comes to books,
He hides the ones that I like best,
That's my 'Precious Princess'.

My brother is daft
When it comes to art,
He just don't understand craft
When he has to make a hat.

My brother is an alien
Making stupid noises,
He thinks he's so angelic
But he's really so annoying.

Emma Shankland (10)
Forehill Primary School

WINTER

W   inter is a silver season,
I   cy icicles hanging from rooftops,
N   ecks wrapped up warm,
T   winkling snow on the ground,
E   njoying the sight of the red robins,
R   obin red is looking for food.

Eve Allan (8)
Forehill Primary School

SCHOOL IS (NOT) COOL

I think about school
As wicked, weird,
Cruel and cool.

It's strange,
It's funny,
It's got a range
Of cool stuff (not).

I hate school,
It's cruel,
It's only cool.

S   is for shyness,
C   is for cruel,
H   is for happy,
O   is for old,
O   is for brains on,
L   is for laziness.

Everyone hates *school,*
The teachers, the pupils,
People who are cool.

The people that do like it
Have got to be weird.

Kirsty Gibson (10)
Forehill Primary School

THE FEEL OF THINGS

I like my furry, fluffy cat, he is so cuddly.
I like the feel of bubbly chocolate melting in my mouth.
I like my soft, cuddly pillow when I go to bed at night.
I like my hard, round leather ball.
I like the hot radiator, it is nice to sit beside.

I do not like the feel of a slimy snake.
I do not like the hairy spiders that crawl on you.
I do not like the feel of the hard, rough crab.
I do not like the feel of the slimy fish.
I do not like the feel of chalk.

Geordan Little (8)
Forehill Primary School

IN THE PET SHOP

In the pet shop there were -

A hundred and one cages full of cats on soft mats,
A hundred and two cages full of bats with furry hats,
And a hundred and three cages full of rats with baseball bats.

In the pet shop there were -

A hundred and one pens full of smelly hogs,
A hundred and two kennels full of crazy dogs,
And a hundred and three tanks with snakes on logs.

In the pet shop there were -

A hundred and one tanks of slimy, yucky snails,
A hundred and two branches packed with fat quails,
And a hundred and three bird cages of snowy owls that wail.

In the pet shop there were -

A cross between a lion and a hippo with a toothache!

I think I'd better go.

Jennifer Solok (10)
Forehill Primary School

THE FEEL OF THINGS

I like the feel of my warm, cosy, comfy and soft slippers on my feet.
I like the feel of my soft, silky, smooth hair running through my brush.
I like the feel of my lovely, smooth, furry dog cuddling in to me.
I like the feel of my fluffy, hairy and squashy teddy that I squash
                                                                          at night.
I like my warm, bouncy and soft bed after a hard working day at school.

I don't like the feel of wet, sloppy, sticky sand.
I don't like the feel of slimy, squashy, gooey slugs.
I don't like the feel of slimy, gooey, sticky snails.
I don't like the feel of spiky, jagged hedgehogs.
I don't like the feel of silent, tickly ants crawling up my leg.

Ainsley McClinton (8)
Forehill Primary School

WHEN I'M . . .

When I'm at home my brother is annoying.
When I'm watching him he sends me out.
When I'm watching TV he always starts fighting.
When I'm playing football he always trips me up.
When I'm eating dinner he always makes me laugh.
When I'm playing with my friends he always chases me.
When I'm playing my PlayStation he always wants my game.
When I'm looking at his homework he takes it off me.
When I'm at my den with my friend he always climbs up and gets us.
When I'm called for dinner we always race down the stairs.

Callum Stevenson (10)
Forehill Primary School

THE SUMMER HOLIDAYS

When the summer holidays come
I burst out the school doors
And shout 'Yippee!'

When the summer holidays come
I like to jump on the computer
And play all day.

When the summer holidays come
I like to play outside with my friends
And race on our bikes.

And that's what I do
When the summer holidays come.

David W Bell (10)
Forehill Primary School

MY STUPID CATS

My cats are so annoying,
They widdle on the floor,
They really do get on my nerves,
They scratch wood off the door.

My cats are so annoying,
They scratch and hiss and shout,
And when they widdle on the floor
The place loses its drought.

But then
In comes Bonnie,
And she's not annoying.

Steven Blackmore (9)
Forehill Primary School

WHEN I LEAVE SCHOOL

When I leave school
    I'll be off forever and ever
    Till the day I die.
    I can go out to play
    Till midnight every day.

When I leave school
    I'll be off forever and ever
    Till the day I die.
    I can stay in bed
    Till whenever I like.

When I leave school
    I'll be off forever and ever
    Till the day I die.
    I won't have to do maths,
    English or French.

When I leave school
    I'll be off forever and ever
    Till the day I die.
    I'll be glad when I leave school.

Natalie Parker (10)
Forehill Primary School

WINTER

W hite snow covers everything,
I   cy patches on the river,
N umb fingers and toes,
T he ice is twinkling on the top of the river,
E verything looks white,
R obin is looking for food.

Ainsley Deans (8)
Forehill Primary School

MY CLASSROOM

My classroom
Has lots of lovely paintings
Hanging on the wall.

My classroom
Has lots of children chatting
And driving the teacher up the wall!

My classroom
Has a very dusty blackboard
Because the teacher writes so much on it.
Sometimes it is interesting
And sometimes I don't know what it is about.

My classroom has lots of jotters
Piled high upon my teacher's desk
But then she sticks her head round
And tells us to be quiet.
Ah silence!

Emma Hunter (10)
Forehill Primary School

WINTER

W hite falling snow on the village ground,
I cicles hanging at the window and the gutter,
N ew season coming and that season is winter,
T ingling cheeks, fingers and noses,
E verything looking as pretty as a postcard,
R oofs like icing on a birthday cake.

Megan O'Lone (8)
Forehill Primary School

THE FEEL OF THINGS

I like the feel of sweet, sugary, bubbly chocolate melting down
                                        on my tongue.
I don't like the feel of rough, sticky sharpenings on my hand.
I like my cosy, silky, warm pyjamas on my skin.
I don't like the hard, sore end of my toothbrush banging off my gum.
I like my bouncy, cosy, warm, comfy bed after school.
I don't like sticky, gooey, wet sand sticking to my feet.
I like my warm, cosy, soft school jumper.
I don't like sticky, slimy jam in a sandwich.
I like my fluffy, furry, soft, cuddly toy.
I don't like dusty, smudgy chalk on my hands.

Scott Cassidy (8)
Forehill Primary School

THE FEEL OF THINGS

I like the feel of cool, smooth, white snow on my hand.
I like the feel of a slimy, small snail on a branch.
I like the feel of hard, brown, dark bark on the tree.
I like the feel of my wibbly, wobbly ear lobe on my hand.
I like the feel of nice smooth, cold ice-cream on my tongue.

I don't like the feeling of a crushed brown, pointy leaf on my hand.
I don't like the feeling of a hard black, sharp stone on my foot.
I don't like the feeling of prickly, spiky hedgehog.
I don't like the feeling of a soft pink flower on my leg.
I don't like the feeling of hard white chalk on my hair.

Callum Dunlop (8)
Forehill Primary School

WINTER

W hirling and whisking goes the snow twirling round,
I t looks like icing all over the grass,
N ipping toes and very cold lips, I hope my toes don't freeze,
T ip-toeing along the grass the lake looks as if it's turned to glass,
E xcited children with red rosy cheeks,
R eally cold children running around in the playground.

Eilidh Hollow (8)
Forehill Primary School

WINTER

W hirling wonderful white snow sweeps across the village,
I cy icicles hanging from the rooftops like glass swords,
N umb feet, fingers and toes are frozen in the cold,
T rembling hands and feet,
E arly morning white as ice,
R eally cold it was.

David Moore (8)
Forehill Primary School

WINTER

W inter is the coldest season,
I ce sparkling on the pond,
N ew season begun,
T hrowing snowballs at each other,
E veryone extremely cold,
R obin redbreast looking for food.

Tobias Kolb (8)
Forehill Primary School

ANIMALS

The cat across the street from me has,
Nasty, vicious claws.
My dog named Dozy wanders all around the house,
All day long sleeping then eating
These silly animals.

My hamster keeps me up all night
Sometimes I wish I could leave him there.
I think there is a rat infestation
At night I hear them scurrying through the rooms
These silly animals.

The kangaroo in the zoo was
Hopping around knocking their heads and falling over.
The penguins squeaking at each other
Diving into the water
These silly animals.

The rhinoceros is in the bushes
Ready to strike.
Oh no, the teacher
The most ferocious one of all!
These silly animals.

Calum Atkinson (10)
Forehill Primary School

THE FEEL OF THINGS

I like my desk, it is smooth and hot.
I like cuddling my fluffy, furry, hairy cat.
I like ice cream, it is fluffy and cool.
I like paper, it is smooth.
I like my bed, it is nice and soft and comfy.

I don't like wet moss, it is hairy and slimy.
I don't like slippy, slimy slugs.
I don't like the radiator, it is hot and lumpy.
I don't like hot metal, it gives you burns.
I don't like wet sick, it is lumpy and sticky.

Andrew Young (8)
Forehill Primary School

MY TEACHER

My teacher really is a pain
She makes us clean dusters in the rain.
She looks out the window
And at the door she shouts
'Look out here comes more.'
Only one problem, this is only Monday!

Next she shouts, 'Be careful those dusters are only new.'
And now I feel like a monkey
Getting shouted at in Glasgow Zoo.

Thank goodness tomorrow is Wednesday
Our breakfast challenge will begin
The only thing I'm dreading is what
The teacher will bring in.

Not my teacher - Mrs McNair!

Gillian Geoghan (10)
Forehill Primary School

THE FEEL OF THINGS

I like the feel of rugs with soft, bumpy and fluffy hairs,
It feels as if I were in the air.
I like the cold and smooth chocolate melting in my mouth.
I like the cold and crunchy carrots getting munched on my teeth.
I cuddle my fluffy, furry teddy when sleeping in the night.
I like the feel of comfy, snug covers and squashy pillows
To relax after a hard day's work at school.

I don't like the feel of slippery, slimy slugs slowly slithering
On the grass, and yucky, watery paint sticking to my hand.
I hate the feel of slippery, squashy snakes twisting around my leg,
And squishy, gooey baking mixture all mixed and sticky too.
I don't like bumpy, rough bark all hard and horrible.

Brogan Murphy (8)
Forehill Primary School

THE FEEL OF THINGS

I like the feel of a snake's skin, slimy and gooey.
I like the feel of a hamster's fur, cuddly and furry.
I like the feel of a fish's scales, smooth and soft.
I like the feel of a dog's fur, cuddly and spiky.
I like the feel of my hair, smooth and wavy.

I don't like the feel of muck, sticky and slippy.
I don't like the feel of rough bark, rough and hard.
I don't like the feel of slushy snow, wet and slippy.
I don't like the feel of spiky nettles, pointed and jagged.
I don't like the feel of my sweatshirt, hot and furry.

Scott Monaghan (8)
Forehill Primary School

THE FEEL OF THINGS

I like the feel of a hard, bumpy, fluffy rug under my bare feet.
I like the feel of smooth, soft, silky wallpaper on my fingertips.
I like the feel of hard, knotty, furry hair running through my fingers.
I like the feel of a smooth, furry dog to cuddle.
I like the feel of a smooth, soft, hard table because it is cold.

I don't like the feel of gooey, slimy slugs going on to my hand.
I don't like the feel of soft, smelly flowers because it goes through
                                        my head and I am sick.
I don't like the feel of soft, shiny fish, they bite my fingers.
I don't like the feel of sloppy, slimy paint, it sticks to my hands.
I don't like the feel of tacky, gooey glue, it sticks my fingers together.

Heather McCallum (8)
Forehill Primary School

THE FEEL OF THINGS

I like the feel of a scaly, silky snake around my neck.
I do not like a tickly ant silently creeping up my leg
But I like the storming, blowing wind in my face.
I do not like the feel of wibbly wobbly, slimy pasta in my mouth.
I really like the feel of a furry, fluffy, cuddly toy to cuddle at night.
I do not like the feel of prickly, pointed barbed wire touching my finger.
I love the feel of my soft and cuddly, fluffy gerbils to play with.
I do not like the feel of freezing water that makes me shiver and chatter.
I like the feel of a smooth relaxing bath water.
I really do not like the feel of rough sandpaper, it makes my bones chill.

Luke Sargent (8)
Forehill Primary School

THE FEEL OF THINGS

I like creamy, drippy, silky chocolate slipping down my tongue.
I like soft, slippy snow under my feet.
I like my cuddly, warm mum when I am cold.
I like my dad's jaggy, spiky beard when he gives me a kiss.
I like the smooth, silky, tickly feeling of my sister's hair when
                                    she bends over me.

I don't like the cold, wet, soaking rain slipping down my arm.
I don't like the sore, wobbly feeling of my tooth coming out.
I don't like the bursting, banging ear infection when I am trying
                                    to get some sleep.
I don't like the nippy, scratch from a cat.
I don't like the cold, freezing water from the tap.

Robbie Hunter (8)
Forehill Primary School

THE SEA CREATURES

The sea is full of wonderful things,
Oh, how I wish I could see them all.
Evil sharks roaming, shipwrecked boats,
Swimming with dolphins and other fish too!
Sea anemones hunting for their food,
Starfish, crabs and shells peacefully lying at
                the bottom of the sea.
Oh! I do wish I could go to the sea!

Samantha Lee (9)
Forehill Primary School

OUR CLASSROOM

Our classroom is
Very big and boring
With brown tables spread all over the room.

Our classroom is
Very noisy with chattering children, chatting all day,
Our teacher stands and shouts some of the day.

Our classroom is
Very annoying sometimes, especially when the
Teacher stands up and natters on and on.

Our classroom is
Very boring, it never excites me any of the time.
I wish our classroom was bright but I suppose it'll never be.

Rebecca Gibson (10)
Forehill Primary School

THE FEEL OF THINGS

I like the feel of bubbly, smooth chocolate melting on my tongue.
I don't like the wet, slippy rain dripping down my face.
I like my soft, bouncy bed because it is comfy.
I don't like tickly, silent ants crawling up my leg.
I like my fluffy, cuddly dog rubbing against me.
I don't like gooey, slippy slugs slithering over my shoes.
I like the feel of soft, slidy snow when I touch it.
I don't like the feel of my brother's tickly hair.
I like my soft, cuddly gran because she spoils me.
I don't like the feel of my wobbly tooth when it is ready to come out.

Hayley Swan (8)
Forehill Primary School

THE FEEL OF THINGS

I don't like tickly, silent ants creeping along my arm.
I don't like slippy, slimy slugs that slither over leaves.
I don't like wet, sticky sand sticking to my feet.
I don't like slippy, slimy fish making my hands all wet.
I don't like smelly flowers, sometimes they make me sneeze.

Neil Shankland (8)
Forehill Primary School

WINTER

W   hite snow is falling.
I   cy icicles hanging from the windows.
N   umb fingers and toes.
T   ingling lips and noses.
E   verything all white.
R   obin redbreast looks for food.

Michelle Jayne Nicol (8)
Forehill Primary School

WINTER

W   hirling snow covering everything,
I   cicles hanging clearer than diamonds,
N   umb fingers and nose,
T   ingling ears and toes,
E   verlasting fun in the snow,
R   ooftops whiter than white.

Steven Morrison (8)
Forehill Primary School

WINTER

W avy ice and whirling snow,
I   cy paths and frosty grass,
N ever had I seen so much snow,
T   emperature changes every day,
E   njoy making snowmen,
R   obins are looking for food to eat.

Laura MacDuff (8)
Forehill Primary School

WINTER

W hite snow falling and whirling,
I   cicles hanging like glass spikes,
N umb fingers, hands and toes,
T   hrowing white snowballs,
E   verything better than the warm summer,
R   obin ready for his big fight to get food.

Craig McGhee (8)
Forehill Primary School

WINTER

W alking in a winter wonderland,
I   ce cream rooftops was what I saw,
N umb fingers and toes as I walked through the snow,
T   iptoe through the snow and hear the wonders of winter,
E   verything white and wonderful,
R   obins nesting in the treetops, all cosy and warm.

Alana Rachel Watt (8)
Forehill Primary School

WHEN THE BELL RINGS

When the bell rings -

Everyone gets out of school and runs before they
                                        can be called back,
Some walk and some scream,
Others are quiet and go slow,
Others drop litter and start to bellow.

When the bell rings -

I sometimes walk and I sometimes run,
It just really depends if I want to have some fun.
Children run around the playground waiting for their mum,
Others go straight home and others don't.

That's what happens in the playground
When the bell rings!

Lyndsay McCabe (10)
Forehill Primary School

IN THE PLAYGROUND

In the playground
    There is always football in the dirt
    And someone surely will get hurt.

In the playground
    There is always a big fight
    And someone always gets a fright.

In the playground
    There are people who always natter
    That are obviously full of chatter.

Connor McPherson (10)
Forehill Primary School

OUR CLASSROOM

Our classroom . . .

Is a pile of unmarked jotters,
A messy library,
A class full of computers.

Our classroom . . .

Is full of talkative children,
Has got wrecked blinds,
A pile of maths books.

Our classroom is . . .

A messy teacher's table,
A blackboard full of work,
A tip.

Garry Johnston (10)
Forehill Primary School

IF I WERE A DOG

If I were a dog I'd chew my bone
and I would eat it upon a stone.

If I were a dog I'd wet my paws
and if I were a dog I'd chase the crows.

If I were a dog I'd clean my dish,
If I were a dog I'd search for my owner's liquorice.

But I'm not a dog, now you know I'm a boy,
Oh, I'd better go to school, you know it's the rule.

Stuart Ritchie (10)
Forehill Primary School

MESSY PETS

Messy Pets

Jaws is messy when he comes out
He brings sawdust and bedding.
That drives me mad.

Messy Pets

At night I sleep and he is awake
Chewing on bars gives me a fright
And very mad at night.

Messy Pets

When he drives me mad I put him out.
He makes the bars go silver
That twinkle in my eye.

Messy Pets

I thought his tooth must hurt
His tooth is very big
When he yawns it gives me a terrible fright.

Messy Pets

In his ball he goes speeding
Like a F1 car. Faster even.
He is really the best hamster I think.

Messy Pets

Jaws can climb stairs really quickly.
I give him his favourite treats
He swallows them quickly.

Greg Templeton (10)
Forehill Primary School

THE THINGS MY FAMILY DO

My mum,
>She works in the bank,
>She taps on the computer,
>And tampers with the paperwork.

My dad,
>He goes fishing two or three times a week,
>He only catches one or two fish,
>But he is happy the rest of the day.

Me,
>I go to school to work and learn,
>I play in the playground with my friends,
>And sit on my chair and quietly work.

Lesley McIntyre (11)
Forehill Primary School

WINTER

W inter is white, wavy and wonderful,
I   cicles like spears all around,
N   umb fingers and toes,
T   ingling lips and nose.
E   xcitement, excitement all around,
R   aring to go to have fun in the snow.

Greg Paterson (8)
Forehill Primary School

WINTER

W inter, whirling white snow is falling to the ground,
I   cicles are left from Jack Frost and houses are like a birthday cake,
N umb noses, lips and toes are all cold,
T   ingling lips and fingers,
E   verything looks so so pretty,
R   ivers are frozen like a big ice rink.

Rosie Eggo (8)
Forehill Primary School

WINTER

W ater covered in ice all over,
I   cicles hanging from the window,
N ew white snow lying silently,
T   winkling snowdrops landing on my nose.
E   xciting things are going on,
R   obins sing their sweet song.

Melanie Stobie (8)
Forehill Primary School

IN MY HEAD

In my head I see myself in water
floating on toast and beans.

In my head I think of being in the ring
beating the champion boxer.

In my head I see myself as a toy
fighting all the other toys and winning.

Bruce MacDonald (10)
Inveraray Primary School

FEELINGS

Happiness is yellow
It tastes like chocolate
and smells like strawberries.
Happiness looks like wee babies
and sounds like birds tweeting.
Happiness is Celtic winning the league.

Laziness is green
It tastes like cold water and Irn Bru
and smells like frozen chips.
It sounds like snoring
Laziness is a sleep.

Sadness is black
It tastes like soap
and smells like rotten eggs.
Sadness looks like sick
and sounds like screaming
Sadness is like getting punched.

Jamie Divers (10)
Inveraray Primary School

ON THE HUNT

Twitching nose
Body in a perfect pose
Watching prey - buffalo, bison.
Keen eyes watch the calf at play
The creature creeps stealthily forward
Then a pounce, then a stampede
Then a death and finally a feed.
At dead of night there comes a howl
The wolves have made a kill.

Kate Stronach (10)
Inveraray Primary School

TREES

Winter trees bare
Under a grey sky
Snow glitters on the branches
Then spring comes to melt the snow
The leaves start to bud and grow
Then the trees are green and full
Waving in the sunny breeze
Then summer comes with warm winds
And the leaves shine with light
But old autumn's coming soon
And nights get colder and the
Leaves start to turn
Red and brown, yellow and gold
Crumpled, crinkled and sad
Then
They
All
Fall
Down

Ben Goodman (10)
Lismore Primary School

SNOW

I love it in the winter
When the snow is knee-deep high
I put on welly boots
And throw snowballs through the sky.

I climb on my sledge
And slide down all the hills
Over bumps and stumps upon the ground
It gives me such a thrill.

My brother comes outside
And builds a snowman with me
The sun comes out so suddenly
And shines upon us three.

Sandy Woods (9)
Lismore Primary School

STAND AND STARE

One day I was fishing with my dad but all he did was stand and stare
I was watching TV with my mum but all she did was stand and stare
When I am not well, all they do is stand and stare
When I eat and sleep but still all they do is stand and stare.

When I go out to play she'll go to the window to stand and stare
When I go to school she will wait to stand and stare
When I'm not working and having a rest they will be there to
                                    stand and stare
I got off the boat with my dad he paid the fare but all he did was
                                    stand and stare.

But why, I think and as I do they will be there to stand and stare
And when I sleep you hear not a peep because all they do is
                                    stand and stare
'Mum, Dad, why do you do this?'
'Because we care
That is why we stand and stare.'

Sam Woods (11)
Lismore Primary School

SNOW ON THE ISLAND

Snow is fun to play in
Snow is very light
Snow is made of little crystals
That glitter shiny bright.

A white, hilly island
In a blue, sparkling sea
Snow on the roads and a huge, big tree
I hope a big pile will not fall on me.

Dad comes out to see me
'Let's snowball fight,' he said
I aim a whopper at my dad
And hit Duncan Brooks instead.

Andrei Cannings (10)
Lismore Primary School

THE UNICORN

I see the most beautiful thing that I have ever seen.
You see a small boy staring up at you.
Your eyes are intense and focused.
My eyes are young and still searching.
My head is full of silly, childish thoughts.
But your head has many wise and wonderful thoughts inside it.
You are the wise, the superior,
You are the unicorn.

Rurigdh McMeddes (10)
Lismore Primary School

To a Cat

To a cat all golden and furry,
To a cat that loves to play,
To a cat that's playful and fluffy,
To a cat I name him Jay.

To a cat that chases mice,
To a cat that plays with me,
To a cat that's very nice,
To a cat I name her Dee.

To a cat that chases birds,
To a cat that plays with toys,
To a cat that feeds on birds,
To a cat I name him Toby.

To a cat that's soft and cuddly,
To a cat that's cute and small,
To a cat that's never muddy,
To a cat I name her Doll.

To a cat that's old and grey,
To a cat that's often ill,
To a cat that has a nap at midday,
To a cat I name him Bill.

To a cat that's young and bouncy,
To a cat that wants to play,
To a cat that's small but jumpy,
To a cat I call her Fay.

To a cat that plays with his ball,
To a cat that sits on the sill,
To a cat that loves his ball,
To a cat I name him Phil.

Andrew McLean (11)
Lochgilphead Primary School

APOCALYPSE

The end of days,
Horror beyond imagination,
Evermore in Hell, evil men scream,
Every friend you ever had,
Never to see Earth again,
Dead.
On the cloud that is Heaven God watches,
Forever damning those who oppose him,
Death to all on Earth,
Always to reside in Heaven or Hell,
You shall not survive,
Said end of days.

Ruaraidh Dobson (10)
Lochgilphead Primary School

MY PONY

My pony, soft and cuddly,
My pony, wet and muddy,
My pony, fast as a cheetah,
My pony, a big fat eater,
My pony, full of grace,
My pony, with a pretty face,
My pony, her name is Candy,
She is the best in all the landy.

Kirsten Lawrence (11)
Lochgilphead Primary School

CHEEKY MONKEY

There's a little, cheeky monkey not far from here,
But when he gets too close to you,
He'll scream in your ear,
And he'll eat all your bananas,
Then steal your pyjamas,
But when you want them back,
He'll just put them in a sack,
So if you see a cheeky monkey,
Don't go near,
Because he'll scream in your ear,
Eat your bananas,
Steal your pyjamas and put them in a sack.

Good luck, getting away.

Jane Cook (11)
Lochgilphead Primary School

SPACE

Space is a wonderful place,
It is not far from the world's face.
Not many people have been there,
But some people just can't bear
The stars are glittering very bright
And the moon is lighting up the night.
All the planets in the sky
So very, very, very high.

Andrea Sutherland (11)
Lochgilphead Primary School

THE GREAT WRESTLER

S   tone Cold Steve Austin is the best wrestler and
T   ears everybody apart
O   n the wrestling ring and he does not let
N   o one beat him on the wrestling ring will someone
E   ver beat him? I don't know.

C   ool Stone Cold Steve Austin is in a match tonight
O   n the wrestling ring with the
L   ight heavyweight champion being 201 pounds
D   'Lo Brown.

Graham Milton (11)
Lochgilphead Primary School

WORLD WAR

Down at the stations where soldiers stand by
Saying goodbye to their children and wives.
The war has started, there's no joy in that
For people will die and never come back.
As every soldier prepares for pain,
As gunshots and bullets fly their way.
This is the war, this is no fun,
For they can't go home until their work has been done.
As countries fight and try to win
They also feel the pain in their enemies' hearts.

Selina Hunter (11)
Lochgilphead Primary School

OPPOSITES

From the biggest whale to the tiniest fish,
From the tallest tree to the smallest plant,
From the longest river to the shortest lake,
From the widest ocean to the narrowest sea.

From the tiniest kitten to the biggest tiger,
From the smallest bird to the tallest giraffe,
From the shortest lizard to the longest snake,
From the thinnest dog to the fattest cat.

Very different they all may be but they
All live together on a planet called Earth.

Gillian Smylie (11)
Lochgilphead Primary School

SPORTS

Golf, football and badminton, these are my favourite sports
I play them all the time.
Especially in the summer.
Football is the best.
Because you can play inside or out.
Badminton is tiring, especially with my friends.
Golf is fun and hard.
I sometimes beat my dad.
But I am still not good enough to beat my friends
These are my favourite sports.

Craig Cowan (11)
Lochgilphead Primary School

THE LITTLE GARDEN GNOME

The little garden gnome
Is quite a cheeky chap,
With old blue and white pyjamas
And a bonnie tartan cap.

In the morning he is still,
But in the night
He gives you a fright
Sticking his tongue out
And trying to bite.

But sometimes I wonder
If he's actually real
Or is it just a dream?

Sarah Dickie (11)
Lochgilphead Primary School

SWEET LIKE ROSES

Golden like daffodils
Red like wine
Sweet like roses
Their smell so divine.

Green as the grass
Blue as the sky
Sweet like roses
For you and I.

Heather Williamson (11)
Lochgilphead Primary School

THE MAN ON THE MOON

Mr Boom is the man on the moon
He's a jolly chap
With a cymbal on his head as a hat
Banana feet walking around the rough surface of the moon
But sometimes you wonder
If there is a Mr Boom?
If someone does live on the moon?
I think it would be Mr Boom.
The water movement is just his shower
The holes are his bowls
I saw him one day he said
'Come and visit me.'
Mum says it was a dream
Or was it . . . ?

Jenna Samborek (11)
Lochgilphead Primary School

FRIENDS

I have lots of friends
Not all of them are in my class
I don't mind much because I see them all at school.

I have lots of friends
I see some when I go riding
Not all my friends are people.

Me and my friends have lots of fun together
That's why I call them my friends.

Liza Connelly (11)
Lochgilphead Primary School

HORSES

H orses are beautiful,
O ver the hill they trot,
R iding them is amazing,
S addles are shining in the tack room,
E very horse is special,
S o why do some people not like them?

Lauren Rutherford (11)
Lochgilphead Primary School

ROBOTS

Robots are wonderful inventions
They have been brought to people's attention,
There are puppies to dancers and even prancers
Robots are cool and some are cruel
Robots are wonderful things.

Struan Thorpe (11)
Lochgilphead Primary School

THE HORSE

The horse was alone
It sat in his big, black home
He sat with a comb.

Kirsty Davidson (11)
Lochgilphead Primary School

SPACE

Space is a place very unknown
Space is a place we'd love to go
Space is a place nobody knows
Space is a place we've never seen
Space is a place I'd like to be.

Michelle Leitch (11)
Lochgilphead Primary School

THE FAT BUTCHER

The fat butcher likes his own sausage
But if everyone comes in they always take his sausage
But then he is upset and said to his wife
'I don't want to sell my sausage any more.'

Craig Bruce (11)
Lochgilphead Primary School

MY RABBIT

My pet rabbit is so cute, playful and sweet,
She hops around the grass, all day having lots of fun,
That's my pet rabbit Barnie,
I love her loads.

Nichola Clark (11)
Lochgilphead Primary School

In The Morning

In the morning I get up
Sometimes it's raining
Sometimes it's not
I have breakfast, tea or coffee
I don't care
I get dressed and go and watch CBBC
I go to school, it's grey and dull
And very, very boring.

Suzanne Holms (11)
Lochgilphead Primary School

Badminton

Badminton is my favourite sport,
I play it every week,
I hit the shuttlecock up in the air
Which lifts me off my feet,
I do my best to hit it back
And I score lots of points,
I love to play badminton so much
And I'm never going to stop.

Danielle Finlay (11)
Lochgilphead Primary School

Football

Football, football I love the sport
Football, football who do you support?
So many to choose from, so many to see
So what team will your favourite be?

Tom Wilson (11)
Lochgilphead Primary School

In A Moment Of Silence

In a moment of silence in Germany I heard
An F22 drop lots of atom bombs.

In a moment of silence in the centre of Germany
I heard the rumble of a small earthquake.

In a moment of silence in Berlin
I heard people say 'A war might start soon.'

In a moment of silence in Bonn
I heard some tanks going to Belgium.

In a moment of silence in north Germany
I heard lots of explosions nearby.

In a moment of silence in south Germany
An army of men march to France.

Michael Murphy (10)
St Columba's Primary School, Oban

In A Moment Of Silence

In a moment of silence in primary 6
I heard my teacher bang on my desk.
In a moment of silence in primary 6
I heard cars zooming outside.
In a moment of silence in primary 6
I heard the trees blowing.
In a moment of silence in primary 6
I heard the wind whistling.
In a moment of silence in primary 6
I heard a girl screaming!
In a moment of silence in primary 6
I heard a lot of talking.

Sean MacMillan (10)
St Columba's Primary School, Oban

Rainforests

R   ain pit-pattering on the dark, forest leaves
A   nacondas nine metres long
I   nsects eating the fallen debris
N   eed more trees for the forest to live
F   ish like stingrays on the riverbed
O   tters diving
R   ivers flowing through the rainforest
E   lephants playing in the shallow water
S   corpions stinging the living things
T   igers roaring at other animals
S   loths climbing up the tall forest trees.

Gavin Hoey (10)
St Columba's Primary School, Oban

Ghosts

I once saw a ghost on my bed
It looked to me like it had no head.
I once saw a ghost in my house
It looked to me like a mouse.
I once saw a ghost in the class
It looked to me it was covered in grass.
I once saw a ghost in my room
It looked to me like an old, dead groom.
I once saw a ghost in the mirror
It wasn't me and it made me shiver.

Jonathon Gillies (10)
St Columba's Primary School, Oban

IN THE RAINFOREST

In the rainforest you can hear the rustles of animals in the bushes
In the rainforest it is as dark as the night sky
In the rainforest you can hear birds singing operatic songs
In the rainforest colourful fish swim in shoals
In the rainforest the monkeys swing from tree to tree
In the rainforest the otters and their babies hunt the fish
In the rainforest the flowers smell of strong perfume
In the rainforest trees are as tall as one hundred buses
                              on top of each other
In the rainforest monkeys swing and play on vines
In the rainforest birds feeding their babies with tasty grubs
In the rainforest tigers hunting down rabbits for their cubs
In the rainforest the canopy is full of birds, leaves and monkeys.

Penny Gillies (9)
St Columba's Primary School, Oban

RAINFOREST

R ainforests are noisy places
A nimals are everywhere
I   n the rainforest it is dark
N oises from everywhere
F orests are scary
O h, look at all the animals
R oots from the trees
E ast, north, west, south, there are trees
S treams are flowing
T rees are very big.

Marco Nicholson (10)
St Columba's Primary School, Oban

IN A MOMENT OF SILENCE

In a moment of silence in a farmyard
I heard the bleating of a newborn lamb
In a moment of silence in a farmyard
I heard the cows grazing in the field
In a moment of silence in a farmyard
I heard the farmer grooming his horse.
In a moment of silence in a farmyard
I heard the scurrying of a dormouse
In a moment of silence in a farmyard
I heard the rabbit burrow a hole
In a moment of silence in a farmyard
I heard the farmers wife calling him for tea.

Gillian Campbell (10)
St Columba's Primary School, Oban

IN THE RAINFOREST

R   ain in the rainforest, tip, tap, tip, tap
A   nimals big and tall and even small
I   nsects very, very small
N   oises in the rainforest are annoying
F   rogs in the rainforest, ribbit, ribbit,
O   ur parrots going squawk, squawk
R   ain in heavenly downpours
E   agles eating monkeys
S   nakes hissing everywhere
T   rees being demolished.

Sean McCowan (10)
St Columba's Primary School, Oban

IN THE RAINFOREST

In the rainforest you can hear
gorillas roaring like they are fighting.
In the rainforest you can hear
the brightly coloured parrots squawking in the trees.
In the rainforest you can hear
the rain tip-tap on the leaves.
In the rainforest you can hear
frogs jumping on the rotten leaves.
In the rainforest you can hear
snakes slithering on the forest floor.
In the rainforest you can hear
trees moving in the wind.
In the rainforest you can see
little bits of light coming through the leaves.
In the rainforest it is really dark.

Ashley Strang (10)
St Columba's Primary School, Oban

THE RAINFOREST

Pitter-patter the leaves go
As the rain falls heavily down,
Letting the ground flood.
As the water fills the ground of the rainforest
The animals climb up to the top of the trees.
While the fishes race across the water
To look for places to hide.

Catriona Campbell (10)
St Columba's Primary School, Oban

RIDING ON A DOG SLED

When I'm on a dog sled
I can feel a breeze in my face
The snow is glistening underneath the sled
It is very cold and icy
The place is very serene
When you're on a dog sled
You can see the huskies' breath
Sometimes it gets too warm
So the huskies have a day off
When you're on a dog sled
You have to run beside the huskies
To make them turn another way
It's great fun on a dog sled.

Laura Sutherland (9)
St Columba's Primary School, Oban

THE RAINFOREST

So many sounds in the rainforest
Rain dripping off the leaves
Pitter-patter
The monkeys swinging from tree to tree
The insects scurrying about in the grass
It's so hot that it's hard to catch a breath
The rain falls so heavily that you'll be soaked in a minute
The trees are so tall you would never imagine it.

Kaireen Moore (10)
St Columba's Primary School, Oban

RIDING ON A DOG SLED

We have a pack of huskies
Their mane is grey or black
When they rest their heads on snow
They sleep on the cold
Or sometimes 'gainst the sack.

If we go or stay at home,
We go and eat and eat
And when we go to sleep
We have some smelly feet.

When we see the ice
We go to hunt some food
We sometimes need some spice
And when we want to go to sleep
It's sometimes cold, so we wear a hood.

Rachel Armstrong (9)
St Columba's Primary School, Oban

MY DREAMS

I was dreaming of a purple sky,
And stars all around me.
The stars were nice and shining bright
There was a boat floating by.
I looked down and saw a tiger
Suddenly parrots were flying all around me
The parrots flew away
I grabbed onto a balloon and floated away and away
In the purple sky.

Kathrine MacNeil (10)
St Columba's Primary School, Oban

RIDING ON A DOG SLED

You feel the wind blowing on your face.
The huskies pull very fast.
I can see the glittering snow.
It is lovely and peaceful on the sled.

I sometimes have to run beside the dogs.
The dogs will turn then.
It is so peaceful, I sometimes fall asleep.
I really like riding on the dog sled.

You can see the huskies breathe.
There is no noise on the dog sled.
The snow is so peaceful out here.
It is so serene on the snow.

I give rides on the dog sled.
They will not pull if it's warmer than -10°c.
We feed the dogs our meat.
It is great on the dog sled.

Ruth Carson (8)
St Columba's Primary School, Oban

IF I HAD WINGS I WOULD FLY TO . . .

If I had wings I would fly to the centre of the sun
If I had wings I would fly to the top of the Empire State Building
If I had wings I would fly to the top of Parkhead to watch Celtic
If I had wings I would fly round the world two times
If I had wings I would fly to the top of K2.

Matt Rippon (10)
St Columba's Primary School, Oban

RIDING ON A DOG SLED

I am riding on a dog sled
On the dog sled the wind blows on your face
Sometimes I fall asleep on the sled
It is very serene
The snow is very glittery
If it gets over minus ten, the huskies lie down
You can see the huskies breath.
Sometimes I have to get off to turn the dogs
The dogs are very strong
The dogs eat a lot of meat
I think the wee puppies are cute
The dogs pull the sled really fast
The dogs like the cold
The dogs don't like the heat
I don't like snowmobiles
It is really peaceful on the dog sled.

Sarah Louise MacPherson (9)
St Columba's Primary School, Oban

THE STARS

Stars are as bright as the sun and the moon
They're all different shapes and sizes
The stars sparkle in the darkness every night
And they glitz when they come
I think I'm getting jealous
Because they are so precious and pretty to me
I hope you like them because they sure inspire me.

Lauren Dickison (10)
St Columba's Primary School, Oban

THE TROPICAL RAINFOREST

The ripple spreads
The water glows
And the river flows through many trees
But please be aware of the tiger!
It lives among those high trees,
With the beautiful coloured leaves.

Have you seen the parrot?
The parrot has charm
And it's a beautiful colour
It flies from tree to tree
Sing a melodious tune.

The rainforest is dark
And the trees are very high
They almost cover the sky
The monkeys swing from tree to tree
Laughing with glee.

The rafflesia is a big flower
And it smells of raw meat
Please don't go near
Because the smell is outstanding.

The rattlesnakes give you shivers
They usually live near the river
And the tarantula
Don't even look at it
It would give you a scare!

Maria Robertson (10)
St Columba's Primary School, Oban

RIDING ON A DOG SLED

Here I am on the sparkling snow
How fast do I go?
I don't know do you?
I will guide the dogs, if I want to turn
I'd better look out for the icy burn.
I go zooming towards the ice
I'm hungry I want something nice
When can I go?
I have got really cold toes
I wonder when the dogs will give up?
When will they? I don't know.
I'm going to win the race
My dogs are the fastest
They'd better watch the pace
It's really slippery.
The dogs don't mind the cold
We're heading for the pit
What's the temperature? If it's low
The dogs don't go slow
They love snow
Oh! Oh! Here comes a walrus
We'd better just go
It is eighty degrees Celsius minus zero
Here comes the polar bear
Look what they wear!
I'm riding on a sled
In the wonderful snow.

Jamie Tonner (9)
St Columba's Primary School, Oban

RIDING ON A DOG SLED

When I get on that dog sled
I always feel like I'm in my bed.
I tell the dogs, faster, faster,
I feel like I'm the demon headmaster.
When I go on that dog sled
I don't know if I'm alive or dead.
I asked my mum pull over there
I think I just saw a polar bear.
Then when the ride comes to an end
I say to the dogs 'Thank you my friends.'
Then after that I give them a bit of meat
I gave them that because they look dead beat.

Craig McFadyen (9)
St Columba's Primary School, Oban

RIDING ON A DOG SLED

We have a pack of huskies
The cutest are the puppies
We go on a sled every day
'It's sure great fun,' they all say.

We always hunt for meat
And we always take a seat
We always have a great, big pack
We don't even need a sack.

We always go for a really great ride
It is not even on a slide
Inuits live in a polar land
It is never covered in sand.

Robert Robertson (9)
St Columba's Primary School, Oban

RIDING ON A DOG SLED

As I go along I feel the wind go by
I see the breath of the huskies
I have to get off to make them turn
And it is so quiet and silent.
I hear the lovely sound of the huskies
It is good fun on a dog sled
If the temperature isn't below minus 10
The husky team will not go.
And the snow glittering and glistening
It is good fun on a dog sled
And as we go along
An icy blast will appear from behind.

Iain MacLean (9)
St Columba's Primary School, Oban

RIDING ON A DOG SLED

It was a cold and frosty morning
And we went on a dog sled
The ice was sparkling
It was so serene.
You can even fall asleep
I had to get off the sled
So I can show the husky dogs which way to turn
And you can see the husky dogs breath
If the temperature is low the dogs won't go
You can see the wind blowing your hair up!

Gavin Owens (9)
St Columba's Primary School, Oban

RIDING ON A DOG SLED

I am riding on a dog sled
On an Arctic landscape.
The breeze is coming to my face.
The hair on my head is gliding to my back.

The snow is glistening as we go by.
Sometimes I get of to guide the dogs round.
The dogs will not go if the temperature is not low.
Polar bears, seals and walrus are what we see.

The sea is grey, blue and black.
I see the huskies breathe in the air.
There are mostly about twelve dogs pulling us.

Stacey Louise MacCormick (9)
St Columba's Primary School, Oban

RIDING ON A DOG SLED

A ride on a sled is great fun.
When the huskies breathe you can see their breath.
The huskies go very fast.
The wind goes zooming past us.
My eyes sparkle when the dogs go fast.
Sometimes I have to get off to turn the dogs.
If it is past ten degrees Celsius the dogs won't go fast.
Sometimes I fall asleep on the sled.

Christopher MacLeod (9)
St Columba's Primary School, Oban

RIDING ON A DOG SLED

It was a glittering sparkling day.
I was outside going for a ride
On the dog sled with my mum.
We were getting the dogs ready to go
When we were going the wind
Was blowing in our faces.
The air was going up our noses.
The snow was going in front of us.
Then I would jump off
And make them turn to go home,
And we would go inside.

Kieran Gallagher (9)
St Columba's Primary School, Oban

RIDING ON A DOG SLED

The dog sled is the best way to travel.
I like going down the hills on the sled.
I like the snow.
I close my eyes on the sled.
Sometimes I jump off the sled.
Sometimes I tumble down the hills.
Sometimes I close my eyes.
Sometimes I fall asleep on the sled.
Sometimes when I go too fast
I feel that I am in Heaven.

Mary Catherine MacIntyre (9)
St Columba's Primary School, Oban

RIDING ON A DOG SLED

On a dog sled we slide along the soft peaceful snow.
With a soft breeze the soft snow splashes in your face.
It is just lovely.
We think that it is the best way to travel
So we go out a lot.
We go out every day.

Karina Hoey (9)
St Columba's Primary School, Oban

RIDING ON A DOG SLED

Dog sleds are very good fun in the Arctic.
They are the best way to travel.
The ice sparkles when the sun is shining on it.
It's so quiet, we take a rest and fall asleep sometimes.
The dogs fall asleep as well.
And I sometimes I have to get off
To make the dogs turn.
I love it when the wind blows in my face.

Simon Anderson (9)
St Columba's Primary School, Oban

THE TEDDY BEAR

This is a poem about a teddy bear
Who belongs to a girl called Claire.
Every night she goes to bed,
With her adorable little ted.
She snuggles in to keep him warm,
They both have dreams from dusk 'til dawn.

Ashley Clark (11)
St John's Primary School, Ayr

COLOURS OF THE RAINBOW

The colour of the blazing sun is yellow.
Yellow is also the colour of glittering stars
That shines in the dark night's sky.
Shining brightly are the lovely sunflowers
In the dark night sky the yellow moon shines down.

Red is the colour of blood coming from a cut.
Juicy strawberries are red and sit in the bowl.
Red presents danger and anger.
The flames that dance in the fire are red.
Poppies that sit in the field, swaying in the wind.
Prickly roses that are given to your loved ones.

White is the colour of soft snow falling on the ground.
Seagulls flying about are white.
The dress of a beautiful bride.
Icing of a cake is white as snow.
The white clouds that float around the sky.
The bones under our skin.
The snow on the peak of a mountain.

Kathleen Maclean (10)
St John's Primary School, Ayr

ELECTRICITY

There was a young girl called Felicity
Who knew how to use up electricity.
She never turned off the power
When she went for a shower
And then Felicity stopped using electricity.

Murray Thomson (11)
St John's Primary School, Ayr

CUDDLY TOYS

I have a cuddly teddy
His name is Eddy

I have a fluffy lion
I called him Brian

I have a stripy zebra
I call her Debra

I have a fluffy dog
His name is Pog

I have a cuddly cat
I called her Pat

I have toys galore
I don't need any more.

Gabriella Gilardi (11)
St John's Primary School, Ayr

FRIENDS

Friends forever
You got to be friends forever
Some people
Out there might be nice
And some
Of them might be bad
So when
You see someone ask if they are nice
That's friends forever
Friends forever.

Antonio Woods (8)
St John's Primary School, Ayr

MY FAMILY

My family are good to play with,
They keep me company.
I have a little brother
And a sister, she's just wee.

Sometimes we go for walks,
We go climbing up the trees.
Sometimes we take the kite,
It goes flying in the breeze.

I play on my bike
While my brother's on his scooter.
Niamh is too small to play
She's just a little looker.

Rochene Mullen (8)
St John's Primary School, Ayr

THE YEAR

January is the time for rabbi,
February is when lovers should be happy,
March is when spring is finally here,
April is when jokes are in the air,
May is when the nights are lighter,
June is when the sun is brighter,
July is popular for vacation,
August is time for the catwalk sensation,
September and its races bring summer to a close,
October is time for Hallowe'en ghosts,
November is Guy Fawkes time of year,
December is for Christmas cheer!

Katy Conlan (11)
St John's Primary School, Ayr

SCHOOL

Some of the teachers are kind of nice
You never see any mice,
That's because the cleaners, clean everything up
The dinner ladies do the washing up
And here's us children just working away
Looking forward to break when we can play
Yeh we'll talk,
And go to the bin for a walk
But it's all part of being at school
When you think about it, it's pretty cool
We get to see our friends
Do swapsies and lends
Some things are fun
And we don't want to run
But then there's maths,
Hard sums and secret paths
I suppose I don't care
Because it's pretty fair
At school!

Gillian Dunlop (11)
St John's Primary School, Ayr

COLOURS OF MY PAINTBOX

Green is the colour of freshly cut grass
The Irish shamrock lying in the fields
The leaves blowing in the trees
And crickets jumping about.

Yellow is the sun blazing onto a hot beach
Bananas lying in the supermarket or in the fruit bowl
Custard over a jam roly poly
The moon and stars glistening all through the night
Sand blowing about on the beach

White is snow falling on Christmas morn
Polar bears having fun in the freezing cold
The milk swirling about in the cereal bowl
Icing covering a birthday cake
A bride coming down the aisle.

Craig Doherty (11)
St John's Primary School, Ayr

SENSE POEM

Rough mountains climbing high into the sky,
covered in heather and long green grass.

Children playing on the beach
while the waves crash against the cliffs.

The smell of seaweed fills my nose
as creeping behind it is the sweet smell of garlic.

The taste of salt from the windy sea air
fills my mouth, mixing it with the sweat
from my upper lip.

Cold water trickling through my fingers
like a worm, nettles on my hands feel sharp.

My body is filled with happiness
while I run through the long grass,
knowing I have the hot sand to play on.

Julia Maltby (11)
St John's Primary School, Ayr

SCHOOL

When it came to the first day of school
I thought it would be really cool,
But later as it got into the day
I just didn't want to stay.
I thought I'd draw a picture of a car
And the teacher would give me a gold star,
Unfortunately I did hard work.
You weren't even allowed a smirk,
When I was doing hard stuff
The teachers were really rough.
After my first day, I thought school was really bad,
And it made me really very sad,
But sometimes in bed at night
When daylight is out of sight
And I'm all tucked in
Bedcovers up to my chin
I think schools have to be there
Even if it does make happiness rare.
We wouldn't be able to use our sight,
Read or even write.
Even when I was in school I didn't draw a car
And the teacher didn't give me a gold star,
Even when I wasn't happy
And I wasn't allowed to be yappy,
And sometimes the teachers were really snappy
School isn't sad,
Because it really isn't that bad.
Even if it's there in different seasons
School is there for fantastic reasons.

Maria Godfrey (11)
St John's Primary School, Ayr

LADYBIRD

Ladybird, ladybird where have you been?
Down in the water in a submarine.
Ladybird, ladybird what did you see?
A jellyfish on the window making faces at me.

Ladybird, ladybird where have you been?
Down to Hollyrood to visit the Queen.
Ladybird, ladybird what did you see?
A greenfly eating leaves off her rose tree.

Ladybird, ladybird where have you been?
Down to Downing Street to visit Tony Blair.
Ladybird, ladybird what did you see?
A whitefly eating his garden chair.

Ladybird, ladybird where have you been?
Up to space to visit Saturn's rings.
Ladybird, ladybird what did you see?
A fat man eating onion rings.

Ladybird, ladybird where have you been?
Down to Hollywood to visit Mr Bean.
Ladybird, ladybird what did you see?
Mr Bean kissing the Queen.

Liam Baird (8)
Sandbank Primary School

PASTA

Sizzle and fizz.
Simmer and bubble.
Splutter and pop.
Sieve and slide.
Slips onto plate.
Slurp and chomp.
Squelch down throat.
Squeeze into stomach.
Slides of empty plate.
Satisfied and full.
Slide onto settee.
Sleep like a squirrel.
Sssss! Snore! Snore!

Ryan Scott (8)
Sandbank Primary School

AMAZON

Andes mountains is where I start.
Moving towards the Atlantic Ocean.
As it passes forests and toucans
Zooming downwards.
Onwards over rocks and sand
Nose-diving towards the horizon.

Gemma Dorward (8)
Sandbank Primary School

THE OLD MAN

There was an old man from Dunoon
Who decided to go to the moon
So he hired a hot air balloon
In the balloon there was a baboon
He didn't notice until he was away from Dunoon.

Everyone in Dunoon knew that he couldn't make it
And he phoned and said that he could not take it.

He landed in Invearay and turned into a fairy
And that was the end for him.

Jennifer Barron (10)
Sandbank Primary School

NETBALL

N is for net score! Score! Score!
E is for enjoy fun! Fun! Fun!
T is for teamwork together! Together! Together!
B is for a break tired! Tired! Tired!
A is for apples yum! Yum! Yum!
L is for Lucozade keeps you well! Well! Well!
L is for leaping to catch the ball! Ball! Ball!

Lesley Skewis (8)
Sandbank Primary School

ANIMALS

A ntelope running and jumping in the field
N its are crawling through the tangled bushes
   looking until the brushes sweep through the hair
I guana rough backed thick tongued scary monsters
M onkey swinging from tree to tree playing with his pet bee
A lligator wide jaws sniping and snapping tail whipping and thrashing
L ion roaring and hunting eating and sleeping *shh!*
S nake slither and slide along the ground stealthily.

Tom Howard (10)
Sandbank Primary School

DOLPHINS

D olphins are sweet as diamonds
O n the waves they jump and dive
L iving sweet and content
P laying with friends always cheery
H appy as penguins on ice
I njured little dolphins caught in
N ets struggling to get free!
S creeching, screaming, for help!

Cara Phillips (8)
Sandbank Primary School

SPORT

S wimming is a sport that keeps me fit
P asta is a food that will keep you healthy
O ranges are fruits full of vitamin c
R iding on my bike makes my legs really strong
T rying to do this is really very easy if you try!

Daniel Fairclough (9)
Sandbank Primary School

THE LEAK IN THE ROOF

The holes in the roof expanding
 Drip, drip, drip goes the leak
  Splash, splash, splash in the bucket
  Splosh, splosh, splosh as the janitor
   Empties the bucket
    But one day
     It turned into a river
      Running down, down, down
       Soon it will wash us away
        I can't wait till that day.

Scott Ferguson (10)
Sandbank Primary School

THE JANITOR

J   anitor goes fixing things all around
A   ll the time I hear no sound
N   ever has he failed to fix
I   f he shouts it's to put down sticks
T   hinking how to fix the roof it leaks all the time
O   nly pausing when he has time even though my poem doesn't rhyme
R   acing around all the time our jani is just brilliant.

Allan Holland (11)
Sandbank Primary School

BABOON IN A BALLOON

A baboon got stuck in a balloon,
He floated up to the moon
He landed on the moon very soon
The balloon popped
And everything stopped.
He went exploring and found it very boring
He fell asleep and started snoring.
When he woke up he was attached to a toe ring
Onto the side of a giant spider
The spider had been drinking cider
He asked the spider for a giant glider
But he didn't have one so he spun a web.
The baboon said 'I want to go to bed'
He slid down the web and into his bed.

Zoe Gray (10)
Sandbank Primary School

THE MAN ON THE MOON

The man on the moon
Carries a silver spoon
To play a little tune lightly, slightly,
Exploring - so boring
He eats a bun
To have so much fun
In the sun.
The sun is hot
It is like a boiling pot
Flying and lying around Mars.

Christine Alder (10)
Sandbank Primary School

A NIGHTMARE

Oh no! Here comes a man
Chasing me with a machete
Aah! there is someone trying
To strangle me with spaghetti.
I keep running
A monster is chasing me
I come to a wall
I feel so small
The monster comes up to me
I hold my breath and close my eyes
Nothing happened!
I opened them
Then I realise it's just my friend Tom.

Andrew Kuchmeister (11)
Sandbank Primary School

THE FLY

There was a fly
Who lives in the sky.
He loved to eat pies.
He was fat
And one day he got caught.
He was fried
And got eaten by a cat.
That was the end of the fly.

Alexis Ritchie (10)
Sandbank Primary School

IN THE NIGHT . . .

I'm all alone,
In this dark wood.
It's going to get me!
I just know it.

It's eerie in the trees.
What was that?
I heard something,
Maybe a ghost.
Probably just wind.

Ahhh!
A scream behind me.
I start to run, quicker
And quicker, it's gaining!
Faster and faster I go,
Eyes watching me everywhere.
It's the arms that hang
Off the trees.
Someone is dead.
I can see them!

A light in the distance,
Getting puffed out.
The adrenaline is rushing
Taking over my blood and veins . . .

Kirsty Gillies (11)
Taynuilt School

THE ANIMAL RACE

I was walking along in the midnight blue
When I met an elephant called Rory McDo.
He screamed in horror as he saw my face
For he was multicoloured and running the animals' race!

He stopped to chat with me for a while,
And warn me of his cousin Albert the crocodile.
After our chat he waved toodaloo
And headed on his way to Timbuktu.

Then after some time I tripped over a lump of slime,
But I was wrong, it was Rory's cousin Albert Frankenstein
He snapped at me with a hungry face
He was the nastiest creature in the animal race.

Some time later
I met Ian a slater.
He said he was the most handsome in the race
When he said that I covered my face.

I told Ian I better get home
He insisted I did not walk alone.
When I got home my face burned red
I waved goodbye and said I had to go to bed.

Ruth Cameron (11)
Taynuilt School

DARK ZONE

Alone alone I feel so aaa-lone.
A heap to share with a sheep to sleep.
My heart feels it should be from the lonely creak
It should rise as a peak.
Deep deep in a heap you might find something to keep.
Blood is like a flood of Coke
Accepts dark and black not red and light.
If you walk dark in the park
You could hear an owl hark.
Your eyes are as large as pies
Just looking for its eyes.
But ahh! I know it's dark and you couldn't cook
So you can't read a book.
This is your dark zone where you're all alone.
Shame isn't it all the pain in the game.
Play by the rules all you fools.
So come if you play all the rules
As long as you don't break a rule.

Jamie Aitken (10)
Taynuilt School

CLASS CLOWN!

You feel so lonely,
So distressed and down.
So by yourself,
You're just the class clown!

Everyone just laughs at you,
They think it's fun.
They think you're nothing,
Just the class clown!

Somehow you live with it,
And carry on.
They think you're enjoying it,
Being the class clown!

Hannah Matheson (11)
Taynuilt School

THE PLANET KIDZ

There is a place where no adult knows
There is a place where no grown-up goes
Where we are as free as birds
And to an adult no kid must say a word

We will get there by Master Blaster
Than a rocket, it is faster
Ten or twelve to each isle,
Bring a Game Boy, it might take a while

We arrive in a place called *Kidz 4 Eva*
Go to school, we will neva!
First, we will take you to *Ice cream City*
It's made of jelly, makes it look quite pretty.

You don't have to say please, thank you,
Or blow your nose
Just let the bogies drip right down to your toes
You can stay up till twelve-thirty,
Never take a bath, just stay dirty!

But then, when you get to *that* age,
When you have to go on to the next stage,
Goodbye, see ya! Be on your way,
Maybe I'll see you some other day!

Mair McTighe (11)
Taynuilt School

INTO THE DARK!

As I slowly walk into the night
I get a fright.
There are faces in the trees
with glinting eyes staring at me.
Blood thirsty bats screech like rats.
One small step feels like five miles.
The rustling wind moves through the trees.
I see a shadow in the distance.
I hide and think what it could be.
A wolf, a goblin or a monster?
It slowly descends towards me.
I shine my torch on it and I find that it is a creature.
The creature goes off into the night.

As if I scared it!

Callum Nicol (11)
Taynuilt School

INSIDE MY WARDROBE

Inside my wardrobe are mice and lice,
Rats and bats and dogs and frogs.

Inside my wardrobe are cats wearing hats,
Bears eating pears and foxes making boxes.

Inside my wardrobe are sinking ships and mouldy chips,
Crickets with tickets and flies with bow ties.

Inside my wardrobe are shoes and socks,
Ticking clocks, mountains and fountains and trees and bees.

That's what's inside my wardrobe!

Kirsten Bergant (11)
Taynuilt School

ON MY OWN

Watch the water deadly still
All on its own as you sit.
She will ask you if you will wait with her.
In the darkness you will see a singing bee,
Da de da da do ne ra ra.
All on your own,
After talking on the telephone.
Waiting calm and cold
Also you're sitting on some mould.
You don't care even if it was a dare.
Something moves quietly
In the water, then
Splash!
You're no longer alone,
But don't cry
It was calm and it
Didn't harm you,
When you were on your own!

Toni Ann Cooke (11)
Taynuilt School

THE COLD DARK NIGHT

I'm in a forest alone at night,
I hear the leaves crunching under my feet.
The wind screeching through the trees,
The howling through the branches.
I feel terrified, with shivers creeping down my spine,
The bags of cold wind sweeping along my face.
My hands shaking side to side and up and down.
The forest is scary - at night.

Fiona Rawcliffe (10)
Taynuilt School

NIGHT VS DAY

All the trees out to grab me,
Howling wolves out to haunt,
Eyes watch,
Faces stare,
Eerie noises coming after me,
Rustling trees.
Rustling bushes.
Just the wind nothing else.
But then I see cats' eyes,
Bats' eyes!
I start to run faster and faster,
Then I see light.
A torch. Who could it be?
'Michelle? Michelle?'
'Mum I'm here!'

Jessica Anna Dalgleish (11)
Taynuilt School

HAUNTED FOREST

You can hear the owls hooting
When you walk through the forest.
You can hear the rustling of leaves
When the wind blows in your eyes.
You see mysterious things.

You feel terrified, cold and very eerie.
Bats fly around, you just think
They're going to bite.

Liam McGukin (10)
Taynuilt School

WALKING IN THE WOODS

As I'm walking through the woods,
I see glinting eyes.
Trees trying to grab me,
Like sharp pointed needles.
Something's moving,
Or was it the wind?
Rustling leaves,
Was it me?
Someone's watching me,
I'm sure.
Shivers down my spine.
Adrenaline pumping as I run,
As I run home.
Something howled,
Help!
Faces in the trees,
Like they're trying to get me.
Shadows moving all around,
Suddenly stops, there's not a sound.

George Holmyard (11)
Taynuilt School

THE PERSON IN MY HEAD

The person in my head tells me to do this and not that
The person in my head has a mind of its own
The person in my head has a party every night to say yey he's asleep
The person in my head and I have a conversation
When I'm bored but it doesn't last for long.

Steven Parr (10)
Taynuilt School

In The Woods ...

As I walk in the dark, scary woods,
I see glinting eyes of demon bats.
As I get deeper into the woods,
I start to see shadows.
I hear wolves howling and owls hooting,
I can hear someone crawling behind me.
Ahh! There's a monster after me.
Just a stray cat.
As I work my way even deeper,
I can hear footsteps behind me,
Getting closer and closer then they stopped.
I can feel someone's hand on my shoulder,
As I turn round, there's a whisper in my ear.
'Do not be afraid.'

Mairi Campbell (11)
Taynuilt School

Table Manners

Get your elbows off the table
Don't point your finger at Aunty Mabel
Wash your hands before you eat
Use a knife and fork, not your feet
Cut your pizza into smaller parts
Keep your fingers off those strawberry tarts
Please and thank you would be nice
I don't think gravy goes well with rice
Take your hat off when you're eating
Don't interrupt when I am speaking
Make sure your mouth's empty before you speak
We had this discussion only last week!

Nina Currie (11)
Taynuilt School

A WALK IN THE WOODS

The eerie sound of the bats.
The owl hoots with all its might.
The trees attack me with frightening faces.
The wolf howls with the wind.
Then I start to run.
The adrenaline pumping through my body.
The demons rumble the ground.
The dark deepens.
No light to guide the way.

Alexander McDonald (11)
Taynuilt School

TAYVALLICH

The best view in Tayvallich,
On sunny days,
The bay glitters like diamonds in the sun,
It's one of the best views,
At night sparkling like rubies,
At that time of night owls hoot happily,
When Cygnets have races,
The horn for the start echoes through Tayvallich,
Everyone is cheering.

After school the play park
Is filled with the joy of children playing,
On weekends it's like a football stadium,
The pitch has lots of cheers as the players score goals,
The people are friendly and helpful,
The wildlife blooms like flowers,
The weather is like four seasons in one day.

Christopher Murdanaigum (11)
Tayvallich Primary School

NEW YEAR'S DAY IN TAYVALLICH

I remember Dad putting on three layers of clothes on New Year's Day
To keep him warm when he jumped in,
Dad running a hot bath for after the big jump,
The sound of rushing water of Dad's warm, hot bath.

I remember walking down the pier before the jump,
Crowds are getting bigger every year,
Counting down 10, 9, 8, 7, 6, 5, 4, 3, 2, 1, splash!
Everyone swimming to get dressed
Dad putting on his jacket, running up to the house for a
                                        lovely warm bath,
Feeling cold and wet.

I remember going to one of Dad's best friend's houses,
Going up the hill to his house,
Me slipping on some ice,
Having a hot drink,
We went to Gran's,
I said, 'Happy New Year,'
Going home to put on dry and clean clothes.

I remember walking down to the pub,
The bay glistening in the sun,
The village so peaceful,
Getting something to eat,
Then a fizzy drink,
Playing with all my friends,
I'm happy to say Happy New Year,
I'm glad I live here.

Sarah Shackleton (10)
Tayvallich Primary School

A Year In Tayvallich

Spring is here,
Baby animals are born on grassy mounds,
Daffodils growing all around,
People happy, the gales have gone,
Getting their boats ready again,
Sunday races starting once more,
The flapping of sails,
Oh who will win?

Summer's here, oh yes it is,
We shout to our mates,
'Hurry up, come to the beach!'
Everyone's hot,
Let's go on our boat,
Let's jump off, let's go for a swim,
Here we are at Cygnets once more,
Toppers, optimists, rowers, oh let's begin.

Summer's gone but autumn came,
A bit colder now,
I like the colours, red, yellow, orange,
It's time now to put the boats away,
The winter gales are on their way,
I'm getting my paints, I'm sitting down, I like painting trees,
And the autumn sky.

Now winter's here, Christmas is coming,
What will I get?
A Game Boy I think, to take on the boat.
The gales are here, the rain has come, I'm stuck inside,
Oh when will spring come?
I'm very happy, spring's here once more.
Baby animals, let's begin again.

Eilidh MacInnes (11)
Tayvallich Primary School

TAYVALLICH

My special place,
Tayvallich on a calm, sunny day in June,
People going here and there, people going everywhere,
People making pancakes and buns,
People going to church when the bells have rung.

My special place,
Tayvallich on a calm, sunny day in June,
Door bells ringing, people cheering for the regatta race,
Hear the waves lashing the boat,
Splish, splash, gurgle, swish!

The sizzling smell from the barbecue,
Stops the race for brunch,
People laughing,
Saying 'Yum, yum,'
People saying, 'Is that a bun?'

My special place,
Tayvallich on a calm, sunny day in June,
Going to the beach,
We all say, 'What a treat.'
Playing with a beach ball, building sandcastles too.

How very lucky I am, why don't you come too?

Bruce Carmichael (11)
Tayvallich Primary School

FISHES

Some fish are blue
Some fish are black
Most fish go forwards,
But others go back.

Some fish are scary
Some fish are not
Some fish are pink
Or purple with a dot.

Some fish are silly
Some fish are not
Not all fish are pink
Or purple with a dot.

Some fish glide
Some fish jump
Some fish land on the sand with a bump.

Some fish are kind
Some fish are not
Some fish swim miles,
But others just a lot.

The only thing in common
That they have all got
They are big, they are small
They are fishes - the lot.

Elspeth MacDonald (9)
Toward Primary School

LITTLE GREEN MEN

He was a very cynical man,
He wouldn't believe a word you say,
He just refused to believe in UFOs
Up until that day.

It was a debate today,
It was on UFOs,
He searched for his seat,
Among the room's many rows.

The chairman stood up,
He began to speak,
'Firstly, I'd like to point out,
About keeping this from the public,
There's been a leak.

One way or another,
People have found out,
And it really is best,
If they don't know what this is about . . .'

The debate went on for two hours,
And finally it came to an end,
But still nothing had been decided,
It was driving him round the bend.

He was walking home late,
It was half-past ten,
He rounded a corner, looked up and saw,
The creatures from Mars, the little green men!

But his memory was wiped,
So if you asked him, 'What was it like?'
He'd say quite surely,
'Get on your bike!'

Ciaran McCrossan (11)
Toward Primary School

THE AZWEEP

The azweep is a colourful creature,
Once I took it to school and it ate my teacher!
The Azweep's arms are yellow and green,
He's really nice but sometimes he's mean,
The Azweep's favourite food is stew,
And his body is a very light blue,
The Azweep's teeth are cotton wool,
Everyone thinks it's very cool,
The Azweep is stuck together with PVA glue,
And his belt is royal gold too,
The Azweep is an alien and he's 7 foot tall,
And he's very, very happy when he's at the annual alien ball.

Rachel Conkey (11)
Toward Primary School

SMILING

People smile when they are happy
And when you laugh too
And when you are sad there
Is always a smile inside you.

When you are being tickled
That's when you smile the most
When you're excited you smile
Even when you're wrapped up in bed.

Liam Johnston (9)
Toward Primary School

MONSTERS

Monsters can be very tall,
Monsters can be very small.
Monsters come in different shapes,
Some monsters even wear big capes.

Monsters wear different gowns,
Some yellow, blue and even brown,
The king of monsters wears a shiny crown,
To annoy you some monsters pull your trousers down!

Monsters can be a bit of a pest,
Because they want you to jump out your vest!
Some people think monsters are bad,
And that can make some monsters mad!

Paul Mayberry (11)
Toward Primary School